CONTEMPORARY WRITERS

General Editors
MALCOLM BRADBURY
and
CHRISTOPHER BIGSBY

E. L. DOCTOROW

IN THE SAME SERIES

E. L.
DOCTOROW

PAUL LEVINE

METHUEN
LONDON AND NEW YORK

For Sebastian

First published in 1985 by
Methuen & Co. Ltd
11 New Fetter Lane, London EC4P 4EE
Published in the USA by
Methuen & Co.
in association with Methuen, Inc.
733 Third Avenue, New York, NY 10017

© 1985 Paul Levine

Typeset by Rowland Phototypesetting Ltd
Printed in Great Britain by
Richard Clay (The Chaucer Press) Ltd
Bungay, Suffolk

British Library Cataloguing in Publication Data

Levine, Paul
E. L. Doctorow. – (Contemporary writers)
1. Doctorow, E. L. – Criticism and interpretation
I. Title   II. Series
813'.54   PS3554.O3Z/
ISBN 0-416-34840-8

Library of Congress Cataloging in Publication Data

Levine, Paul.
E. L. Doctorow.
(Contemporary writers)
Bibliography: p.
1. Doctorow, E. L., 1931–
– Criticism and interpretation.
I. Title.
PS3554.O3Z78   1985   813'.54   85-4938
ISBN 0-416-34840-8 (U.S.: pbk.)

CONTENTS

GENERAL EDITORS' PREFACE

The contemporary is a country which we all inhabit, but there is little agreement as to its boundaries or its shape. The serious writer is one of its most sensitive interpreters, but criticism is notoriously cautious in offering a response or making a judgement. Accordingly, this continuing series is an endeavour to look at some of the most important writers of our time, and the questions raised by their work. It is, in effect, an attempt to map the contemporary, to describe its aesthetic and moral topography.

The series came into existence out of two convictions. One was that, despite all the modern pressures on the writer and on literary culture, we live in a major creative time, as vigorous and alive in its distinctive way as any that went before. The other was that, though criticism itself tends to grow more theoretical and apparently indifferent to contemporary creation, there are grounds for a lively aesthetic debate. This series, which includes books written from various standpoints, is meant to provide a forum for that debate. By design, some of those who have contributed are themselves writers, willing to respond to their contemporaries; others are critics who have brought to the discussion of current writing the spirit of contemporary criticism or simply a conviction, forcibly and coherently argued, for the contemporary significance of their subjects. Our aim, as the series develops, is to continue to explore the works of major post-war writers – in fiction, drama and poetry – over an international range, and thereby to illuminate not only those works but also in some degree the artistic, social and moral assumptions on which they rest. Our wish is that, in their very variety of approach and emphasis, these books will stimulate interest in and understanding of the vitality of a living literature which, because it is contemporary, is especially ours.

Norwich, England   MALCOLM BRADBURY
                                                  CHRISTOPHER BIGSBY

PREFACE AND ACKNOWLEDGEMENTS

E. L. Doctorow is a remarkable phenomenon among contemporary American novelists: a serious writer who is also popular; a political writer who is also a stylist; an original writer who is highly eclectic; a historical writer who invents the past. In this book I want to follow Doctorow's progress as a novelist by tracing the development of certain themes that recur in his work: the relationship between history and imagination; between élite and popular culture; between political content and experimental style. The effort is worth it, I think, not only because of the excellence of Doctorow's fiction but because of what it tells us about the state of modern American culture.

Yet this effort is not without its problems. 'The trouble with E. L. Doctorow,' observed Nicholas Shrimpton, 'is that he's twice the man you expect him to be.'[1] Shrimpton was referring to the fact that Doctorow writes novels which are both socially concerned and stylistically experimental. These two categories of fiction – realism and modernism – have traditionally been considered mutually exclusive. As Diane Johnson has put it:

> The special trial sent to Doctorow is to be not only righteous but an artist, thought since Victorian times to be antithetical; either the artist must 'sit as God holding no form of creed, / But contemplating all,' in the words of Tennyson's poem, or do a little peace marching, but to try to do both together is to start with a special handicap, like a sack-runner in a regular race. Doctorow is an artist struggling in a message sack, or a messenger beguiled by a sackful of artist's playthings – possibilities of language and form – but all the same he runs a swift race.[2]

The critical consensus that these two categories must be kept apart is difficult to understand. Social vision and formal experimentation have gone hand in hand throughout the evolution of

American literature: from Melville and Whitman through Dos Passos and William Carlos Williams to Mailer and Robert Lowell. 'To call a novel political today is to label it,' Doctorow has said, 'and to label it is to refuse to deal with what it does. My premise is that the language of politics can't accommodate the complexity of fiction, which as a mode of thought is intuitive, metaphysical, mythic.'[3] In American fiction, the mythic and metaphysical have been accommodated traditionally in the type of narrative called the romance. Richard Chase used the phrase 'poetry of disorder' to describe the way in which American reality was refracted in the work of writers like Hawthorne, Twain, Fitzgerald and Faulkner.[4] According to Doctorow himself, he is writing in the same romance tradition as Hawthorne.

The time to write this book was made possible by a sabbatical semester granted by the English Institute at the University of Copenhagen. The research was facilitated by Carl Pedersen and by Karen Kirk Sørensen and the staff of the American Library in Copenhagen. The manuscript was corrected with a discerning eye by Annette Wernblad. My debt to other critics is evident in the text but I am especially grateful to E. L. Doctorow who generously discussed his work with me in a series of interviews. He has given me permission to quote from these interviews and from his work as well. Richard Trenner and Ontario Review Press have also granted permission to quote from their critical anthology, *E. L. Doctorow: Essays and Conversations*. An earlier version of chapter 3 of this book appeared in *Dutch Quarterly Review of Anglo-American Letters*, 11 (1981–2).

The author and publisher would like to thank the following for permission to reproduce copyright material: Macmillan, London and Basingstoke, and Random House for extracts from *The Book of Daniel*, *Ragtime* and *Loon Lake*; Russell & Volkening for extracts from *Welcome to Hard Times*; International Creative Management for extracts from *Big as Life*.

Copenhagen, Denmark, 1984   PAUL LEVINE

A NOTE ON THE TEXTS

Page references for quotations from E. L. Doctorow's works are to the Bantam paperback editions, unless otherwise stated. The following abbreviations have been used:

HT *Welcome to Hard Times*
BL *Big as Life* (New York: Simon & Schuster, 1964)
BD *The Book of Daniel*
R   *Ragtime*
DD *Drinks Before Dinner*
LL *Loon Lake*
LP *Lives of the Poets* (New York: Random House, 1984)
EC *E. L. Doctorow: Essays and Conversations*, ed. Richard Trenner (Princeton: Ontario Review Press, 1983)
I   My (unpublished) interviews with E. L. Doctorow

1

POLITICS AND IMAGINATION

> The principle which interests me . . . is that reality isn't
> something outside. It's something we compose every mo-
> ment. The presumption of the interpenetration of fact and
> fiction is that it is what everybody does – lawyers, social
> scientists, policemen. So why should it be denied to
> novelists?[5]

Writers and critics do not agree on many things but there
appears to be a consensus that American literature has under-
gone a crisis in the past two decades. Philip Roth's famous
lament, expressed in 1961, that contemporary reality was
constantly outstripping the novelist's imagination has been
echoed in many quarters. John Barth spoke of 'The Literature
of Exhaustion' while Ronald Sukenick complained that 'What
we think of as the novel has lost its credibility – it no longer tells
what we feel to be the truth as we try to keep track of ourselves.
There's no point in pushing ahead with fiction: we might as
well write autobiography and documentary, or social criticism
and other how-to books.'[6]

Beginning in the 1960s the American writer faced the kind of
imaginative crisis identified by Doris Lessing as 'the thinning of
language against the density of our experience'.[7] The result was
a literature pulling in opposite directions towards a greater
concern for objective reality and a deeper obsession with
literary self-reflexiveness. Under pressure from the density of
contemporary experience some writers moved to the hybrid
forms of the 'non-fiction novel' and the New Journalism. I'm
thinking of such works as Truman Capote's *In Cold Blood*,
Norman Mailer's *The Armies of the Night*, Joan Didion's
Slouching Towards Bethlehem and James Baldwin's *The Fire*

Next Time. Feeling the thinning of language, others turned to black humour, paranoid visions and a kind of linguistic guerrilla warfare – for instance, Joseph Heller's *Catch-22*, Thomas Pynchon's *The Crying of Lot 49*, Ken Kesey's *One Flew Over the Cuckoo's Nest* and William Burroughs's *Nova Express*. Aware of the exhaustion of literary forms, still others like John Barth, John Hawkes, Robert Coover and Kurt Vonnegut explored the vein of reflexive and fabulistic writing we now call post-modernist. Perhaps Vonnegut spoke for them all when he wrote in *Slaughterhouse-Five:* 'everything there was to know about life was in *The Brothers Karamazov*, by Feodor Dostoevsky. "But that isn't *enough* any more."'[8]

But about the same time that writers like Barth and Sukenick were advising their contemporaries to leave realism to the social scientists, semiologists and historians were beginning to question the traditional distinctions between history and fiction. In different ways, Roland Barthes and Hayden White attacked the special status of history as representation of reality by noting the similarity between the linguistic structures and rhetorical strategies of historical and imaginative writing. It seemed that there was no privileged view of the past. History did not hold up a mirror to reality any more than fiction did. Both were constructed by a particular narrative vision in which facts never spoke for themselves.

Recently, the social historian Herbert Guttman pointed to yet another crisis in the contemporary writing of American history: the failure of scholars to reach an audience beyond their own limited professional membership. Guttman attributed this to the inability to create a viable alternative to the discredited old Progressive synthesis which dominated the writing of history until the 1950s. In recent years, he pointed out, exciting new areas have been opened up in the history of previously 'silent' groups like blacks, women and the working class. But an emphasis on quantitative research and micro-historical studies has tended to fragment our understanding of American history and reduce its intelligibility. Thus, while aspects of the American past look different, '*American history* itself does not look different. And that is the problem.' So, Guttman concluded: 'A new synthesis is needed, one that incorporates and then transcends the new history.'[9]

These gloomy thoughts were stimulated by Guttman's participation in a panel discussion at the American Writers Conference in 1981 of the question 'Have Writers Discarded History?' Interestingly enough, another panel member was E. L. Doctorow, a novelist who certainly has not discarded history. Indeed, in a 1978 interview, Doctorow explained why history had once again become important to writers of fiction:

Well, first of all, history as written by historians is clearly insufficient. And the historians are the first to express skepticism over the 'objectivity' of the discipline. A lot of people discovered after World War II and in the fifties that much of what was taken by the younger generations as history was highly interpreted history. And just as through the guidance and wisdom of magazines like *Time*, we were able to laugh at the Russians' manipulation of their own history – in which they claimed credit for technological advances that had clearly originated in other countries, and in which leaders who had fallen out of favor were suddenly absent from their texts – just around that time, we began to wonder about our own history texts and our own school books. And it turned out that there were not only individuals but whole peoples whom we had simply written out of our history – black people, Chinese people, Indians. At the same time, there is so little a country this size has in the way of cohesive, identifying marks that we can all refer to and recognize each other from. It turns out that history, as insufficient and poorly accommodated as it may be, is one of the few things we have in common here. I happen to think that there's enormous pressure on us all to become as faceless and peculiarly indistinct and compliant as possible. In that case, you see, the need to find color or definition becomes very, very strong. For all of us to read about what happened to us fifty or a hundred years ago suddenly becomes an act of community.

And the person who represented what happened fifty or a hundred years ago has a chance to say things about us now. I think that has something to do with the discovery of writers that this is possible. (*EC*, pp. 58–9)

Doctorow was calling attention to one of the most remarkable developments in recent fiction: the creation of a new kind of historical novel. The renewed interest in history, in part a reaction against the excessive privatization of fiction in the 1950s and in part a response to the political and cultural events of the 1960s, grew during the 1960s with the publication of such varied works as John Barth's *The Sot-Weed Factor*, Thomas Berger's *Little Big Man*, Bernard Malamud's *The Fixer* and William Styron's *The Confessions of Nat Turner*. If fiction was moving in the opposite directions of a greater emphasis on both reality and imagination, then for many writers history became a vehicle for mediating between the two. This concern for historical recreation was shared by a wide spectrum of writers, from orthodox modernists like Styron, Mailer and Gore Vidal to orthodox post-modernists like Barth, Pynchon and William Gass. It may be too much to argue that history has become the organizing principle of recent fiction, like Marxism in the 1930s and Existentialism in the 1950s. But it is not too much to suggest that novelists are providing the new synthesis that Herbert Guttman found missing in contemporary historiography.

This new historicizing fiction appears to be an international phenomenon. One thinks of established figures like Grass, Márquez and Solzhenitsyn as well as younger ones like Thomas Kenneally, Timothy Findley and D. M. Thomas. Indeed, Martin Green has called this international movement 'the most promising development of the last decade or more'. According to Green, novelists like John Fowles, John Berger and Doctorow combine historical perceptions with modernist methods to recreate an epoch from a contemporary viewpoint. The result challenges not only our traditional view of history but the conventional notion of the historical novel as well.

'This is an aesthetic kind of historical fiction,' Green noted; 'the writing is notably elegant, and the writer's most necessary qualifications are taste, tact, and erudition.'[10]

Yet not all contemporary novelists approach history from the same perspective: modernists and post-modernists exploit the past in radically different ways. Both Doctorow and Robert Coover, for instance, have written 'revisionist' texts about the trial and execution of the Rosenbergs. In Doctorow's *The Book of Daniel* and Coover's *The Public Burning* the Rosenbergs are treated similarly as pathetic but complicit scapegoats in some anthropological ritual. But whereas Coover invents outrageous situations for actual figures in order to portray the hysteria of the McCarthy era, Doctorow creates his own characters and immerses them in history to suggest something larger about American radicalism in the twentieth century. Thus in Coover's novel, the public burning itself – the execution of the Rosenbergs – takes place in Times Square, the Mecca of hype and entertainment. For Coover, politics in America is packaged as show business and the execution is depicted as an orgiastic celebration of the corrupt national character. In dealing with post-war America, *The Public Burning* transforms history into myth. Similarly, the climactic scene of *The Book of Daniel* takes place in that other symbol of debased mass culture, Disneyland. But Doctorow's exploration is more resonant historically because the final attempt to retrieve the past occurs in the place which has already abolished history and translated it into popular mythology. This opposition between a critical and a corrupted historical perspective runs through the novel and becomes its main theme. At the end of *The Book of Daniel* we are released from history only by embracing it.

*

We can see how history operates in Doctorow's work by turning to his most popular novel. In *Ragtime* there is a wonderful description of Sigmund Freud's visit to the United States in 1909. The purpose of Freud's visit was to accept an honorary degree from Clark University – the first official recognition of his endeavours. As Doctorow recounts it, the trip was a fiasco. Freud's disciples took him to see the sights of New York but the great man was not impressed. 'What oppressed him about the New World was its noise. The terrible clatter of horses and wagons, the clanking and screeching of streetcars, the horns of automobiles.' They drove to the Lower East Side, the centre of Jewish immigrant life in America, where Freud could not find the toilet he so desperately needed. 'They all had to enter a dairy restaurant and order sour cream with vegetables so that Freud could go to the bathroom' (R, p. 42). Finally, the party went to the amusement park at Coney Island where Freud and Jung took a boat trip together through the Tunnel of Love. 'The day came to a close only when Freud tired and had one of the fainting fits that had lately plagued him when in Jung's presence' (R, p. 43). But the worst was yet to come:

A few days later the entire party journeyed to Worcester for Freud's lectures. When the lectures were completed Freud was persuaded to make an expedition to the great natural wonder of Niagara Falls. They arrived at the falls on an overcast day. Thousands of newly married couples stood, in pairs, watching the great cascades. Mist like an inverted rain rose from the falls. There was a high wire strung from one shore to the other and some maniac in ballet slippers and tights was walking the wire, keeping his balance with a parasol. Freud shook his head. Later the party went to the Cave of Winds. There, at an underground footbridge, a guide motioned the others back and took Freud's elbow. Let the old fellow go first, the guide said. The great doctor, age fifty-three, decided at this moment that he had had enough of America. With his disciples he sailed back to Germany on the *Kaiser Wilhelm der Grosse*. He had not really gotten used to the food or the scarcity of American public facilities. He believed the trip had ruined both his stomach and his bladder. The entire population seemed to him over-

powered, brash and rude. The vulgar wholesale appropriation of European art and architecture regardless of period
or country he found appalling. He had seen in our careless
commingling of great wealth and great poverty the chaos of
an entropic European civilization. He sat in his quiet cozy
study in Vienna, glad to be back. He said to Ernest Jones,
America is a mistake, a gigantic mistake. (*R*, pp. 43–4)

This passage from *Ragtime* provides a convenient point to
enter Doctorow's work because it contains three essential
characteristics that we shall find in all his writing. First of all,
Doctorow's fiction is rooted in history. Each of his major
novels deals with a significant moment in the American past:
the settling of the West in *Welcome to Hard Times*; the
transformation of American life at the turn of this century in
Ragtime; the trauma of the Great Depression in *Loon Lake*;
and the legacy of political radicalism and repression in post-
war America in *The Book of Daniel*. Taken together, these
books form a mosaic of American society from the closing of
the frontier to the end of the Vietnam war.

Yet each of these novels is not simply a faithful recreation of
a historical event but rather an imaginative revisioning of a
historical epoch. *Welcome to Hard Times* imagines the life and
death of an archetypal Western town; *Ragtime* weaves real and
imaginary figures into a tapestry of modern American culture;
Loon Lake explores the American myth of success at the
critical moment when its assumptions were being tested by the
Depression; *The Book of Daniel* transforms an actual event –
the trial and execution of the Rosenbergs – into a meditation on
post-war American radicalism. In each case, Doctorow is more
concerned with imaginative truth than with historical accu-
racy. That is, he is concerned with what *truly* happened rather
than with what *really* happened. Thus it does not matter
whether Freud and Jung did, in fact, take a boat trip through
the Tunnel of Love at Coney Island in 1909. Doctorow's
description reveals in a witty image a psychological truth about
their relationship. Private persons and facts are transformed in

their essence when they enter the public realm. In this connection, Doctorow observed in an interview:

> I'm under the illusion that all my inventions are quite true. As, for instance, in *Ragtime* I'm satisfied that everything I made up about Morgan, for instance, or Ford, is true, whether it happened or not. Perhaps truer because it didn't happen. And I don't make any distinction any more and can't even remember what of the events or circumstances in *Ragtime* are historically verifiable and what are not. (*EC*, p. 69)

Second, Doctorow's revisioning of history reveals a concern with form as well. What was new about *Ragtime*, he once suggested, was not that it used historical figures as fictional characters but that it created a narrative distance that was somewhere between the intimacy of fiction and the remoteness of history: 'a voice that was mock historical – pedantic'.[11] This search for a narrative voice appropriate to each novel is part of the quest for the right fictive form: the process whereby the artist distances himself from his material. 'I don't write autobiography or autobiographical fiction,' Doctorow has insisted. 'I don't take characters directly from my own life or experience. I put them through several prisms.' These prisms are necessary 'to filter myself from my imagination in order to write'.[12]

Doctorow's concern for form has led him to fracture both chronology and narration in order to create the necessary energy for his fiction.

> Beginning with *Daniel*, I gave up trying to write with the concern for transition characteristic of the nineteenth-century novel. Other writers may be able to, but I can't accept the conventions of realism any more. It doesn't interest me as I write. I'm not speaking now of a manifesto – but of the experience of the writer, or at least this writer. You do what works. Obviously, the rhythms of perception in me, as in most people who read today, have been transformed immensely by films and television. (*EC*, p. 40)

These experiments with discontinuous narrative and multiple narrators might suggest a connection with self-reflexive post-modernist writing but Doctorow rejects the identification. 'I'm opposed to that view,' he has insisted. 'I think art and life make each other. Henry Miller said, "We should give literature back to life." I believe that. I believe more than that' (*EC*, p. 38).

Third, each of Doctorow's novels is political in that it addresses in some significant way Freud's judgement that America is a 'gigantic mistake'. By this I do not mean that Doctorow shares Freud's judgement but rather that his fiction describes the gap in American life between its ideals and its reality. He has said of American society:

> It seems to me we are, at least on paper, supposed to be different from, or better than, we are. And that kind of irritation confronts us all the time and has from the very beginning. The Constitution was a precipitate of all the best Enlightenment thinking of Europe, and it's really quite a remarkable document. That we don't manage to live up to it is the source of all our self-analysis. (*EC*, p. 57)

Consequently, it is not surprising to find in Doctorow's fiction an obsession with the idea of justice.

> There is a presumption of universality to the ideal of justice – social justice, economic justice. It cannot exist for a part or class of society; it must exist for all. And it's a Platonic ideal, too – that everyone be able to live as he or she is endowed to live; that if a person is in his genes a poet, he be able to practice his poetry. Plato defined justice as the fulfillment of a person's truest self. That's good for starters. (*EC*, p. 55)

Yet in his fiction the pursuit of justice is never resolved: those who try to redress an injustice by an act of vengeance are often destroyed. Apparently, the idea of justice, like the idea of truth, lies beyond human grasp. 'Of one thing we are sure,' concludes the narrator of *The Book of Daniel*. 'Everything is elusive. God is elusive. Revolutionary morality is elusive. Justice is elusive. Human character' (*BD*, p. 54).

It is tempting to trace Doctorow's social and aesthetic concerns back to his upbringing and education. He was born into a Jewish family in New York City in 1931 and 'grew up in a lower middle-class environment of generally enlightened, socialist sensibility' (*EC*, p. 53). After graduating from the prestigious Bronx High School of Science, he attended Kenyon College where he majored in philosophy and studied literature with the famous critic, John Crowe Ransom. After a year of graduate work in drama at Columbia University and two years in the army, he returned to New York to begin his writing career. During the early lean years he worked at a variety of editorial jobs. By the time he quit to write full-time he had become a top executive at the Dial Press.

Clearly, Doctorow's family background has deeply influenced his development as a writer but in ways which are more complicated than they seem at first glance. His grandfather and father were secular Jews committed to ideas of progress and socialism. But his grandmother and mother were both politically and religiously conservative. Consequently, 'there's always been this tension in the family which is, I think, quite reflected in what I've done' (*I*). Yet Doctorow sees these conflicting positions not as contradictory but rather as complementary. Thus his identification with radical Jewish humanism is broad: it embraces both the political progressivism of Emma Goldman and the cultural conservatism of Sigmund Freud. 'Whether they were radical or not, there was some sort of system of thought – a humanist critique, a social or political skepticism, whatever you want to call it – that had to come from their inability to be complacent or self-congratulatory' (*EC*, p. 54). This 'humanist critique' is fundamental in everything he has ever written.[13]

But there is another source for his radical scepticism. Coming of age in the early 1950s, Doctorow is part of what has been called the silent generation. Irving Howe once described them as 'the generation that did not show up', meaning that they fell between the political radicalism of the 1930s and the cultural radicalism of the 1960s.[14] Doctorow would agree. 'My generation has known, without having to go through the experience of the Thirties, the dangers of ideology as they are applied to fiction and poetry,' he observed. 'We have learned that lesson. We were taught that lesson' (*I*). But the lesson has had its costs in the lack of a shared set of convictions. 'It's the fate of my generation that we've never shared a monumental experience. We think of ourselves as loners' (*EC*, p. 37). The effect of this detachment is reflected in the isolation experienced by his protagonists and in the genuine ambivalence expressed in his novels. 'In every work I've ever done,' Doctorow has remarked, 'I've always heard the answers to whatever assertions are made by anybody' (*I*).

Because he has chosen to deal with explicitly political issues in his fiction, Doctorow has sometimes been labelled an ideologue. But, as I have already suggested, he is aware of the dangers of ideology for art. He knows that the artist's political convictions 'cannot be brought into the writing. They must come out of the writing' (*I*). Moreover, his own scepticism about the efficacy of simple political solutions is evident in each of his novels. 'But surely the sense we have to have now of twentieth-century political alternatives is a kind of exhaustion of them all,' he has explained. 'No system, whether it's religious or anti-religious or economic or materialistic, seems to be invulnerable to human venery and greed and insanity' (*EC*, p. 65).

Doctorow's ideas about the nature of literature and the role of the artist were perhaps best stated in an essay he published in 1977 entitled 'False Documents'. The essay begins with a comparison of two sentences, one from a newspaper article and one from a novel, which stem from the different realms of fact and fiction and represent the conflicting powers of '*the regime*' and of '*freedom*'. By '*the power of the regime*' Doctorow means our acquiescence to the authority of brute facts which goes by the name of realism; by '*the power of freedom*' he means the ability of the imagination to subvert that authority. 'There is a regime of language that derives its strength from what we are supposed to be and a language of freedom whose power consists in what we threaten to become. And I'm justified in giving a political character to the nonfictive and fictive uses of language because there is a conflict between them.'

But '*the power of the regime*' is like the emperor's new clothes. It is a product of our perception of reality and not reality itself. As such, it may be changed as our consciousness is transformed. 'What we proclaim as the discovered factual world can be challenged as the questionable world we ourselves have painted – the cultural museum of our values, dogmas, assumptions, that prescribes for us not only what we may like and dislike, believe and disbelieve, but also what we may be permitted to see and not see' (*EC*, p. 17). Thus reality is something that we invent and the notion that fact and fiction belong to separate realms is itself an invention.

This interpenetration of fact and fiction undermines the distinction between scientific and imaginative writing. Historians and sociologists borrow the techniques of fiction in the name of the regime of language. The characteristic devices of historical narrative turn out to be closely linked to the fictive conventions of realism. So Doctorow is 'led to the proposition that there is no fiction or nonfiction as we commonly understand the distinction: there is only narrative' (*EC*, p. 26).

The discovery that the boundary between fact and fiction was itself fictional was made by the first novelists, by Cervantes and Defoe, who presented their own inventions as factual accounts. Doctorow adopts Kenneth Rexroth's phrase 'false documents' to describe these fictions. In American literature a similar strategy was used by Hawthorne and Melville. Hawthorne described his own work as romance which attempted to connect past history and present reality through an act of imagination. He claimed that his romances occupied 'a neutral territory, somewhere between the real world and fairyland, where the Actual and the Imaginary may meet, and each imbue itself with the nature of the other'.[15]

The qualities that Hawthorne imputed to the romance come down to us in the mainstream of American literature from

Hawthorne and Melville through Faulkner and Fitzgerald to the fabulators of the present day. But a contemporary practitioner like Doctorow, with his abiding political interests, has more in common with such writers as Grass and Márquez than he does with most other American post-modernists. What this international group of writers shares, in addition to a belief that all history is contemporary history, is a faith in the subversive significance of the imaginative act. In 'False Documents' Doctorow put his position this way:

> Novelists know explicitly that the world in which we live is still to be formed and that reality is amenable to any construction that is placed upon it. It is a world made for liars and we are born liars. But we are to be trusted because ours is the only profession forced to admit that it lies — and that bestows upon us the mantle of honesty. (*EC*, p. 26)

2

FICTION AND FORMULAS

It was only after I had written those first two books, for example, that I developed a rationale for the approaches I had taken – that I liked the idea of using disreputable genre materials and doing something serious with them. I liked invention. I liked myth. (*EC*, p. 36)

Doctorow's first two novels were, in a sense, products of a coincidence. This is appropriate for a writer who has come to believe that all writing originates in accident. By the late 1950s Doctorow had already decided upon a career as a novelist but he had not as yet found his own style. At the same time that he was trying to write a novel about a college youth, he was employed as a manuscript reader. Soon, however, the scripts caught his imagination more than his novel:

I don't imagine I would have written *Welcome to Hard Times* if I'd not been working at that film company and reading lousy screenplays week after week. I had no affinity for the genre – I'd never been west of Ohio. I thought Ohio *was* the West. Oh, as a kid I'd liked Tom Mix radio programs and maybe I went to see a few movies; but, really, I had no feeling for Westerns. But from reading all these screenplays and being forced to think about the use of Western myth, I developed a kind of contrapuntal idea of what the West must really have been like. Finally one day I thought, 'I can lie better than these people.' So I wrote a story and showed it to the story editor, Albert Johnson, who was by now a friend, and he said, 'This is good. Why don't you turn it into a novel?' And so I did. (*EC*, pp. 33–4)

One can speculate on why a young writer would give up a

novel based at least in part on personal experience for one which was purely imaginative. After all, Doctorow had been a college student but he had never been out West. But a major stimulant, aside from the liberating feeling of working strictly from imagination, may have been provided by the popular genre itself. As Philip French has noted,

> The Western is a grab-bag, a hungry cuckoo of a genre, a voracious bastard of a form, open equally to visionaries and opportunists, ready to seize anything that's in the air from juvenile delinquency to ecology. Yet despite this, or in some ways because of it, one of the things the Western is always about is America rewriting and reinterpreting her own past, however honestly or dishonestly it may be done.[16]

In choosing the Western genre, Doctorow was already beginning his revisioning of American history. Indeed, the West was an appropriate place to begin because of its central place in our understanding of America's development. From Crèvecoeur to Frederick Jackson Turner, observers have pointed to the significance of the frontier in shaping a specifically American character. Turner went so far as to argue that the particular qualities of American individualism, democracy and nationalism were the fruits of the frontier experience. But the West had a decisive impact on the American imagination as well. Edwin Fussell has traced the origins of American literature to the national fascination with the frontier. As reality and idea, the West both shaped and was shaped by the American imagination. Yet the West we recognize today is an *imagined* West, formed by its recreation in a thousand films and stories. 'The simple truth is that the American West was neither more nor less interesting than any other place, except in mythology or in the swollen egos of Westerners, until by interpretation the great writers – all of whom happened to be Eastern – made it seem so.'[17]

In recent years the ambiguous relationship between the myth and reality of the frontier has been further clarified. Alan Trachtenberg has shown how the frontier myth became an ideological weapon in the development of monopoly capitalism at the end of the nineteenth century. 'As myth and as economic entity,' he argued, 'the West proved indispensable to the formation of a national society and a cultural mission: to fill the vacancy of the Western spaces with civilization, by means of incorporation (political as well as economic) and violence. Myth and exploitation, incorporation and violence: the processes went hand in hand.'[18] The West as imaginative and natural resource, as landscape and commodity, gained in importance as America was transformed into an industrial nation. By the beginning of the twentieth century, Western enterprises were already controlled by Eastern corporations. At the same time, the myth of the frontier was preserved in the popular imagination and transformed in the nostalgic elegies to the receding wilderness by writers like Faulkner and Hemingway or in the celebration of traditional values by film-makers like John Ford and Howard Hawks.

The Western may take many forms but it adheres to a single formula. Both plot and place are unchanging elements in a fixed formulation. John G. Cawelti has identified the perennial locale as a 'symbolic landscape' which structures the enduring encounters between civilization and wilderness, old world and new, East and West.[19] Out of these conventional elements Doctorow created his first novel. But, as he suggested, *Welcome to Hard Times* evolved contrapuntally from his experience with the genre. The result is a work in which both the traditional values of the frontier myth and the conventional character of the Western formula are neatly turned inside out.

Welcome to Hard Times deals with the death, rebirth and final destruction of a Western town, Hard Times, in the years before the closing of the frontier. The novel begins magnificently with the arrival of a legendary outlaw known as the Bad Man from Bodie who proceeds to pillage the town and murder most of its inhabitants. The narrator, Blue, is one of the few survivors of the calamity and, having failed to stop the Bad Man, he decides to stay and try to rebuild the town. Together with Molly, a whore who had been mutilated by the Bad Man, and Jimmy Fee, a boy who had been orphaned by him, Blue establishes a new makeshift family and sets about rebuilding their lives by rebuilding the town. But Blue knows that renewed prosperity will eventually bring back the Bad Man; only this time, he feels, they will be ready for him. Like a classical tragedy which pits character against fate, the novel moves inevitably towards its final confrontation.

Blue knows that the human capacity for self-destruction is one of the natural elements with which men must contend on the frontier. 'Bad men from Bodie weren't ordinary scoundrels, they came with the land, and you could no more cope with them than you could with dust or hailstones' (*HT*, p. 7). But he retains his faith in the power of civilization to tame the most destructive natural elements, even the Bad Man from Bodie. Despite his experience to the contrary, he continues to believe in the positive myth of a pioneer society dedicated to promise and progress.

Thus *Welcome to Hard Times* deals with the classic Western theme of conflict between nature and civilization. But here the wilderness is not redemptive and society is not civilizing. The landscape is flat and barren, its only apparent redeeming feature is the ore which the miners try to extract but even this turns out to be illusory.[20] 'Like the West, like my life,' Blue confesses, 'The color dazzles us, but when it's too late we see what a fraud it is, what a poor pinched out claim' (*HT*, p. 186). In Doctorow's version of the West, nature is not landscape but commodity; and when it turns out to be a 'poor pinched out claim' then the social stability of the town is threatened and the civilized veneer of the frontier is destroyed.

Similarly, the pioneers are neither cowboys nor farmers but petty entrepreneurs whose futures are controlled by Eastern business interests which actually own the land. The leading citizen in the reborn town is a bar keeper named Zar who learns that there is more money to be made in running a brothel than in tilling the soil. 'Farmers starve,' he discovers, 'only people who sell farmers their land, their fence, their seed, their tools . . . only these people are rich. And that is the way with

27

everything' (*HT*, pp. 63–4). Like the others who have gone West, Zar is driven by faith in the American dream. But the dream of success, like the myth of the frontier, is built upon a system of mystifications. The illusion of wealth, like the delusion of progress, urges men onward in pursuit of their fantasies. The West becomes the dreamland of capitalism, the very blankness of the landscape inviting men to project their dreams upon it. But the westward march of civilization proves as unstable as the dream of success that fuels it. A state official says:

> 'If a man files a claim that yields, there's a town. If he finds some grass, there's a town. Does he dig a well? Another town. Does he stop somewhere to ease his bladder, there's a town. Over this land a thousand times each year towns spring up and it appears I have to charter them all. But to what purpose? The claim pinches out, the grass dies, the well dries up, and everyone will ride off to form up again somewhere else for me to travel. Nothing fixes in this damned country, people blow around at the whiff of the wind. You can't bring the law to a bunch of rocks, you can't settle the coyotes, you can't make a society out of sand.' (*HT*, pp. 141–2)

Blue knows that the West is a 'poor pinched out claim' but that does not prevent him from harbouring illusions like everyone else. Yet Blue's optimism is a form of self-deception. 'Well now Blue I always liked you,' someone tells him. 'If you was hanging by your fingers from a cliff you'd call it climbin' a mountain' (*HT*, p. 77). Both Blue and Molly know that the Bad Man from Bodie will return one day but while she puts her trust in the mechanism of revenge he places his faith in the vehicle of progress. In other words, whereas she believes that history can only be repeated he hopes that it can be changed.

Thus *Welcome to Hard Times* may be read not only as a debunking of the frontier myth but as a meditation upon history. While the novel is informed by 'a relentlessly revisionist spirit', as Arthur Saltzman has suggested (*EC*, p. 76), it is finally governed by an almost classically tragic view of history. Blue begins with an optimistic faith in the efficacy of progress but in the course of writing his narrative he comes to understand the cyclical nature of his story. Just as Hard Times rises phoenix-like from its own ashes, built from the decaying lumber of another ghost town, so the Bad Man, eventually killed by Blue, is resurrected in Blue's adopted son, Jimmy Fee. The cycle is not merely closed but repeated. 'Do you think, mister, with all that settlement around you that you're freer than me to make your fate?' Blue asks the reader. 'Do you click your tongue at my story? Well I wish I knew yours. Your father's doing is in you, like his father's was in him, and we can never start new, we take on all the burden: the only thing that grows is trouble, the disasters get bigger, that's all' (*HT*, p. 187).

Doctorow draws upon the biblical idea of generational burden but his version of history never becomes mechanically deterministic. Instead, his characters are caught in the dialectic of possibility and necessity. Blue can never resolve the conundrum of whether we make or are made by history. Could Molly, who predicts the final catastrophe, really have known what was coming, he asks, or did it come because she knew it? 'Were you smarter than the life, or did the life depend on you?' (*HT*, p. 149). In the end he can only conclude that we are as much victims of our illusions as of historical necessity. 'Nothing is ever buried,' he says, 'the earth rolls in its tracks, it never goes anywhere, it never changes, only the hope changes like morning and night, only the expectations rise and set' (*HT*, p. 214). Yet Blue's acknowledgement of the blinding power of illusions cannot prevent him from expressing one last hope in the midst of the final destruction of the town: 'And I have to allow, with great shame, I keep thinking someone will come by sometime who will want to use the wood' (*HT*, p. 215).

Beyond its interest in myth and history, *Welcome to Hard Times* reveals a concern for the act of writing itself. Blue is protagonist not by virtue of his prowess with a sixgun but by virtue of his need to write. Because he keeps the town's books

29

he is called the mayor. His authority is in his authorship. Blue writes down his story in the same ledger in which he has kept the town's records. In fact, he writes his narrative as he is dying over the fading accounts of the town's legal transactions: a palimpsest which symbolizes the process by which fact is transformed into fiction. Blue recognizes the provisional nature of his art. 'I scorn myself for a fool for all the bookkeeping I've done,' he writes; 'as if notations in a ledger can fix life, as if some marks in a book can control things. But there is only one record to keep and that's the one I'm writing now, across the red lines, over the old marks. It won't help me nor anyone I know. "This is who's dead," it says. It does nothing but it can add to the memory' (*HT*, pp. 187–8).

The reflexive nature of the novel suggests the insufficiency of language in the face of reality. Blue is expressing not only his own frustration over the inadequacy of his narrative but perhaps also Doctorow's misgivings about the ability of fiction to convey the truth about life. 'I'm losing my blood to this rag,' Blue says of his journal, 'but more, I have the cold feeling everything I've written doesn't tell how it was' (*HT*, p. 203). This question of the expense of life in the creation of art is one to which Doctorow will return in both *The Book of Daniel* and *Loon Lake*.

Already in this first novel we can see the outlines of concerns which will occupy the author in his later fiction. Blue's narrative written over the town's records in his ledgers suggests the model for the kind of 'false document' that will occupy a central place in his later novels. The revising of the frontier myth reflects the 'revisionist' spirit that will inform his continuing treatment of American history. The exploitation of the Western formula anticipates the more elaborate explorations of popular culture. Even the themes of the elusive character of truth and the complex nature of justice will turn up again and again. As Doctorow recalled:

Welcome to Hard Times was crucial to me for a couple of reasons. First, it showed me my strength, which was *not* autobiographical writing. Somehow I was the kind of writer who had to put myself through prisms to find the right light – I had to filter myself from my imagination in order to write. The second thing I learned was that all writing begins by accident. Eventually it will come around to who you are, it will find some essence, but the *start* of a book is necessarily contingent; you can't plan it. If I had not worked as a reader and gotten angry at what I was reading, I would not have written that particular novel. (*EC*, p. 34)

Welcome to Hard Times was published in 1960, the year that John F. Kennedy expanded the Turner thesis to include outer space and proclaimed the New Frontier as the slogan of his political campaign. The contrast between Kennedy's optimism and Doctorow's pessimism is clear but it was perhaps inevitable that the novelist would pursue his interest in popular forms by turning to science fiction. As Philip French has noted, 'Science Fiction and the Western are at once complementary and antithetical forms. Both are concerned with teaching lessons to the present through a rewriting of the past or by extrapolations of current tendencies projected into the future.'[21]

Big as Life, published six years later, bears some resemblance to *Welcome to Hard Times*. Both begin with the sudden appearance of a disruptive stranger and both end with scenes of apocalyptic destruction. Moreover, both deal with the crisis experienced by a community with the coming of an alien force, revealing the vulnerability of our civilized status and exposing the myths by which society holds itself together. Finally, common to both novels is a protagonist who becomes a recording instrument, a surrogate for the writer himself. What Wallace Creighton in *Big as Life* shares with Blue is his sense of the importance of his role as witness. In words that might have been written by Blue, Creighton, a professor of history, thinks: 'Whatever is happening, however dreadful it may be, I've got to concentrate on the job at hand, which is to get it down for what it is. Even if it's the day of judgment' (*BL*, p. 153).

Big as Life begins with the sudden appearance in New York harbour of two giant humanoids caused by the kind of unprecedented accident that is common in science fiction tales. Existing in their own space and time, the immobile couple loom like new icons over the city, challenging the system of assumptions on which ordinary life is based. For the alien presence not only threatens the existing social order but undermines the fundamental faith in science and religion which supports law and order.

The novel describes the reactions of individuals and groups as well as governments to this new presence which quickly becomes incorporated into the social fabric. At first, Creighton is impressed with the social will for survival. 'All of the superb machinery of our social system,' he writes, 'exists for the sake of the individual. It is no lie. One cannot help being thrilled by the virtually automatic engagement of every self-protective capacity of our civilization' (*BL*, p. 61). When martial law is declared, Creighton joins NYCRAD, the consortium of military, governmental, scientific and religious agencies that is formed to deal with the emergency. His job is to write a history of NYCRAD but he soon learns that its main function is to maintain public order so as to preserve itself.

> There seemed to be growing numbers of public relations and mass media executives in the halls. Their vocabulary depressed him. They spoke of morale control and the manipulation of public attitudes . . . but the essential idea in PR's approach to this objective was to promote NYCRAD itself, to build the image of NYCRAD as a protective and confidence-inspiring instrument of the public good. The self-serving logic in this Wallace found terrifying. (*BL*, p. 89)

Creighton comes to understand that NYCRAD has an existence separate from the needs of the people it was created to serve. It is a mystifying colossus – 'Like our friends in the harbor' (*BL*, p. 89). But he discovers that NYCRAD finally poses more of a threat to survival than the alien creatures do. For NYCRAD's secret function is, like that of Marcuse's one-dimensional society, to accommodate people to the very terrors of the status quo: 'it is meant to engineer tranquillity; it is meant to make the giants part of our way of life, to bring them into the community of fond and familiar things in our daily life. Right? So that nobody panics, so that society can keep working' (*BL*, p. 152). When Creighton learns of NYCRAD's plans to wantonly destroy the passive giants, he joins a group of rebels who are organizing against the increasingly totalitarian corporate state.

Though he is not the narrator, Creighton bears a close resemblance to Blue in *Welcome to Hard Times*. A middle-aged, monk-like man, he finds it difficult to balance faith and reality. 'As a historian, Creighton had turned gray trying to reconcile his natural optimistic nature with the dark depressing data of his profession' (*BL*, p. 12). Like Blue, he is plagued by hope and the compulsion to record reality. 'I keep the books,' he explains. 'I write down what happens' (*BL*, p. 137). Thus he too is caught between his roles as actor and witness. But the historian is given an *alter ego* in the person of a jazz musician named Red who together with his girl-friend Sugarbush represents another way of dealing with reality. Whereas Creighton lives very much inside the established system, Red and Sugarbush live on its fringes almost as outlaws, using the system for their own ends. Red's fanatical dedication to his art and the couple's passionate devotion to life contrast with Creighton's intellectual detachment. 'There's no choice,' Red tells him. 'You make believe that there is some order and that what will happen is up to you' (*BL*, p. 143). Creighton is struck by the sheer vitality of his two young friends, as big as life as the two giants in the harbour. 'You know, it seems to me that you two are inviolate,' he tells them. 'I mean you don't give in to the huge demeaning conditions of life' (*BL*, p. 140). Their decision to have a baby in the midst of catastrophe proves their commitment to life and provides the novel with a note of muted hope.

With its predictable plot, lifeless characters and confusing resolution, *Big as Life* is the problem child among Doctorow's novels. In contrast to his first book, it fails to subordinate its political vision to its imaginative structure or to exploit the possibilities of the popular formula in an original way. Finally, it is the only one of his novels to lack a distinctive narrative voice and to be told in a straightforward third-person narrative. No wonder then that Doctorow has virtually disowned *Big as Life* and has refused to allow it to be reprinted. 'Unquestionably, it's the worst I've done,' he has said. 'I think about going back and re-doing it some day, but the whole experience was so unhappy, both the writing and the publishing of it, that maybe I never will. It's my *Mardi* . . .' (*EC*, p. 37).

With the publication of these first two novels, Doctorow had completed his apprenticeship as a writer. His future fiction would be larger, deeper and more original but it would retain elements from his early work. The concern for history and myth, for narrative voices and 'false documents' which characterizes *Welcome to Hard Times* will turn up again. Similarly, the engagement with social issues that is central to *Big as Life* will be repeated in the later fiction. Even the use of *alter egos* like Wallace and Red will return in an elaborated form in both *Ragtime* and *Loon Lake*. 'It was only after I had written those first two books,' Doctorow has said, 'that I developed a rationale for the approaches I had taken' (*EC*, p. 36). That rationale, involving a concern for both social analysis and narrative innovation, would serve as the basis for the major fiction to come.

3

FICTION AND RADICALISM

> But I think that all writers in all nations operate as children do of families whom they love and hate and try to distinguish themselves from and somehow reform at the same time. And I would put a nation's artists in that category – as loving and tortured children. (*EC*, p. 57)

Nothing in Doctorow's earlier work quite prepares us for the extraordinary achievement of *The Book of Daniel*. Where the first two novels began as experiments in a popular genre, this third novel takes its starting point in contemporary history. As Doctorow explained:

> In the late Sixties I found myself thinking about the Rosenberg case, and it seemed to me that the more I found myself thinking about it, I saw that it was something I could write. And not knowing why or how or what conclusions I was going to come to, I started to write that book and discovered I could hang an awful lot on it – not only the explicit and particular story of two people who were trapped in this way, but also the story of the American left in general and the generally sacrificial role it has played in our history. (*EC*, p. 61)

The late 1960s witnessed the culmination of the remarkable political resurgence that had begun in 1960 with the student sit-ins in Greensboro, North Carolina, against segregation and the student demonstrations in San Francisco against the House Committee on Un-American Activities. As the student protests grew into a national movement expressed in new organizations like SNCC and SDS, a new generation of young radicals appeared who challenged not merely the American power structure but the left-wing political establishment as well. The rise of the New Left was the beginning of a new chapter in the history of American radicalism. As Irving Howe wrote in 1965:

> A major shift or shake-up of 'power relations' seems in prospect for the intellectual world. For the first time in several decades, the generation of intellectuals associated with the thirties – a generation bound together by common problems, experiences, and quarrels – seems in danger of losing its dominant position in American intellectual life. That it has kept that position for so long and through such a bewildering series of political-intellectual changes, is itself extraordinary. But now there is beginning to appear in the graduate schools, and near the student and civil rights movements, a younger generation of intellectuals and semi-intellectuals, perhaps not as well equipped dialectically as the older leftists, semileftists and ex-leftists, and certainly not as wide ranging in interest or accomplished in style, yet endowed with a self-assurance, a lust for power, a contempt for and readiness to swallow up their elders which is at once amusing, admirable, and disturbing. Thinking of themselves as 'new radicals,' these young people see as one of their major tasks the dislodgement of the old ones; and they are not inclined to make precise distinctions as to the differences of opinions among the old ones. A *Kulturkampf* seems in prospect, and one in which, I must confess, my own sympathies would be mixed.[22]

Howe was not the only sympathetic observer on the Left who watched this generational struggle with pained ambivalence. In *The Agony of the American Left* (1969), Christopher Lasch described the limited political perspective of the new movement. With its origins in middle-class alienation, it was largely a student movement which defined political issues in personal terms. Since it was motivated more by a subjective heroic ideal than by an objective social analysis, the New Left vacillated between despair and defiance as it oscillated between radical nihilism and revolutionary romanticism. The result was a movement that was generous in its instincts but often self-destructive in its actions. Similarly, in *The Armies of the Night*, Norman Mailer recounted his own experiences as a witness and participant in the 1967 march on the Pentagon which Doctorow would also use in his novel. According to Mailer, the domestic struggle over Vietnam was the first phase of a new civil war between armies separated by class, generation and ideology. Though Mailer's sympathies were with the young insurgents, he felt himself alienated from their arrogant anti-intellectualism, their ignorance of history and their mindless wastefulness. They were, in Leslie Fiedler's pregnant phrase, 'dropouts from history' who felt disconnected from the past.[23] Jerry Rubin, the generation's most celebrated dropout, declared:

> The 1950s were the turning point in the history of Amerika. Those who grew up before the 1950s live today in the mental world of Nazism, concentration camps, economic depression and Communist dreams Stalinized. . . . Kids who grew up in the post-1950s live in a world of supermarkets, color TV commercials, guerilla war, international media, psychedelics, rock 'n' roll and moon walks. . . . This generation gap is the widest in history. The *pre*-1950s generation has nothing to teach the *post*-1950s.[24]

But awareness of the generation gap indicated that young radicals were existing in a vacuum, without a sense of the past or a connection to the larger society. Tom Hayden, founder of SDS, observed that becoming a radical 'was like giving birth to yourself'.[25] When the enthusiasm waned at the end of the decade as America showed little sign of revolutionary change, the New Left fell as spectacularly and suddenly as it had risen, the victim of factional disputes and its own internecine warfare. Having attempted to abolish history, the new radicals became its victims instead. As William O'Neill remarked: 'When the New Left started it made much of the difference between it and earlier radicals. It was open, undoctrinaire, independent where they had supposedly been conspiratorial, dishonest, and sectarian. But in scarcely more than eight years the New Left recapitulated practically the whole history of American radicalism.'[26]

It is against this turbulent background that Doctorow fashioned his third novel. *The Book of Daniel* is a meditation on American politics in the form of a novel, an imaginative revisioning of the radical movement which attempts to bridge the generation gap and reconnect the new radicalism to its history. It is not simply a fictional account of the Rosenberg case but a threnody on 'the agony of the American left'. In the final analysis, as Doctorow has suggested, the book is not about the Rosenbergs but about the *idea* of the Rosenbergs. Only by comprehending this can we come to terms with the moving ending of the novel and its allusion to the biblical Daniel and another time of repression and hope.

Doctorow's choice of the Rosenberg case as the point of departure for his exploration of American radicalism is crucial. For no other single event reflects the betrayal of radical hopes and the paranoia of Cold War politics as clearly as the controversial trial and execution of Julius and Ethel Rosenberg for atomic espionage. As Leslie Fiedler noted in 1953 there were actually two Rosenberg trials: one, little remarked, in which the pair was convicted and sentenced to death for transmitting state secrets to the Soviet Union, and a second, involving a desperate two-year attempt to reverse the verdict or commute the sentence, which became an international *cause célèbre* akin to the earlier Sacco–Vanzetti trial. This second 'trial' was transformed by both sides into Cold War propaganda, with the Rosenbergs depicted alternatively as helpless victims of the class struggle and as diabolical agents responsible for the Korean War. That the Rosenberg case remains a subject of bitter controversy after three decades testifies to its continuing historical and symbolic resonance.

But there is a *third* Rosenberg case beyond the two which involved questions of guilt or innocence, and this is the subject of Doctorow's novel. It involved more a social rite than a jury trial. As Doctorow has explained, 'the specific dramatic interest I had was solely in terms of what happens when all the antagonistic force of society is brought to bear and focused on one or possibly two individuals, what kind of anthropological ritual is that?' (*EC*, p. 61). Here it matters little that Doctorow has changed some of the facts of the case: that the Rosenbergs are now called the Isaacsons; that their two sons have been transformed into a brother and sister, Daniel and Susan; that the crucial witness against them has been changed from a family member, David Greenglass, to a family friend, Selig Mindish. It also matters less whether the accused are innocent or guilty – in the novel Daniel never finds out – than that they have been selected as scapegoats in a ritual drama beyond their comprehension. As a knowledgeable reporter tells Daniel: 'Shit, between the FBI and the CP your folks never had a chance' (*BD*, p. 228). The implications of this ritual suggest the themes of the novel. In describing the protest against the execution of the Rosenbergs, Fiedler provides us with an insight into the plight of the Isaacsons:

The final protest that existed behind all the others based on stupidity or malice or official dogma was the human one. Under their legendary role, there were, after all, *real* Rosenbergs, unattractive and vindictive but human; fond of each other and of their two children; concerned with operations for tonsillitis and family wrangles; isolated from each other during three years of not-quite-hope and deferred despair; at the end, prepared scientifically for the electrocution: Julius' mustache shaved off and the patch of hair from Ethel's dowdy head (and all of this painfully documented by the morning papers in an America that can keep no secrets); finally capable of dying. This we had forgotten, thinking of the Rosenbergs as merely typical, seeing them in the context of a thousand other petty-bourgeois Stalinists we had known, each repeating the same shabby standard phrases. That they were individuals and would die they themselves had denied in every gesture – and we foolishly believed them.

In the face of their own death, the Rosenbergs became, despite themselves and their official defenders, symbols of the conflict between the human and the political, the individual and the state, justice and mercy; and this symbolic conflict only those who knew they were guilty could fully appreciate.[27]

Here is Doctorow's theme: the Isaacsons are 'symbols of the conflict between the human and the political, the individual and the state, justice and mercy'. Moreover, they come to symbolize the legacy that one generation leaves another: the legacy of the Cold War on the one hand and of the Old Left on the other. The subject of the novel is this legacy, Daniel's legacy, and that is why it is Daniel's book. 'DANIEL'S BOOK: A Life Submitted in Partial Fulfillment of the Requirements for the Doctoral Degree in Social Biology, Gross Entomology, Women's Anatomy, Children's Cacophony, Arch Demonology, Eschatology, and Thermal Pollution' (BD, p. 318).

In an interview, Doctorow provided an insight into how the book was constructed and, not incidentally, what it means:

I started to write the book in the third person, more or less standard past tense, third person novel, very chronologically scrupulous, and after 150 pages I was terribly bored and I realized – in fact, that was a moment of great despair in my life because I thought if I could really destroy a momentous subject like this then I had no right to be a writer. That moment when I threw out those pages and hit bottom as it were I became reckless enough to find the voice of the book which was Daniel's. I sat down and put a piece of paper in the typewriter and started to write with a certain freedom and irresponsibility and it turned out Daniel was talking and he was sitting in the library at Columbia University and then I had my book. (EC, p. 62)

The finished novel is neither a standard third person narrative nor chronologically scrupulous. Rather its fractured time and vivid language reflect the narrator's own sense of dislocation and outrage: this is very much Daniel's book and it contains his feelings of pain and hostility. Though he describes himself as looking 'cool, deliberately cool' on the first page of the novel, it does not take the reader long to discover that he is anything but detached. As he tells us later, his involvement with his sister Susan 'has to do with rage' (*BD*, p. 224). Indeed, rage is his ruling emotion until the end of the novel when aggression gives way to compassion and alienation gives way to sympathy. This movement is reflected in the chronological organization of the novel. We begin on Memorial Day 1967, which commemorates the war dead, and move through Halloween, the night of the witch hunt, to Christmas, the season of rebirth and fellowship. It is in this context, as we shall see, that we can understand the three endings offered for the novel.

There is another way of comprehending the novel's chronological structure. Historically, it oscillates between the early 1950s and the late 1960s: that is, between the height of the Cold War and the decline of the Old Left, on the one hand, and the depths of the Vietnam war and the rise of the New Left, on the other. In other words, we are confronted with the dual legacy of the Cold War and the Old Left, the twin inheritance of repression and radicalism that haunts post-war America. Daniel explains it this way:

> The Berlin Wall is not a wall. It is a seam. It is a seam that binds the world. The entire globe is encased in lead, riveted bolted stripped wired locked tight and sprocketed with spikes, like a giant mace. Inside is hollow. Occasionally this hot lead and steel casing expands or cracks in the heat of the sun, and along the seams, one of which is called the Berlin Wall, a space or crevice appears temporarily that is just big enough for a person to fall through. In a world divided in two the radical is free to choose one side or the other. That's the radical choice. The halves of the world are like the spheres of Mengleburg.[28] My mother and father fell through an open seam one day and the hemispheres pressed shut. (*BD*, p. 278)

If the radical choice is one part of the radical legacy then it is understandable why Daniel feels ambivalent about this dubious inheritance. The seam that binds the world also divides it into two opposing halves that are mirror images of each other (just as the Isaacson trial and the Moscow trials are mirror images of each other). The so-called free world may not be as free as it proclaims but the so-called revolutionary world is certainly not very revolutionary either. Daniel recalls E. H. Carr's analysis of Stalin's triumph as the victory of nationalist over revolutionary forces, leading to the betrayal of progressive movements in Spain, Germany and the Soviet Union itself. 'Thus, to those critics who see in Stalin the "Genghis Khan" he was called by Bukharin, or the extreme paranoid he is sorrowfully admitted to have been by today's Soviet leadership, we must say: no revolution is betrayed, only fulfilled' (BD, p. 66).

The radical who must choose between these two tainted positions is faced with a tragic dilemma. Necessarily, it seems, every commitment must involve betrayal. Daniel knows that his parents were written out of the Communist Party within twenty-four hours of his father's arrest. 'Quickly and quietly erased out of existence' (BD, p. 138). Though his parents never publicly acknowledge this desertion, Daniel imagines his mother thinking, 'Communists have no respect for people, only for positions' (BD, p. 219).

But Daniel realizes that this betrayal involves self-deception as well. If, as he is told, a radical is no better than his analysis, then his parents were guilty of faulty analysis. His father was an idealist who could not distinguish between the splinter political groups at CCNY and the mainstream of American life. Paul Isaacson's failure to make the 'violent connection' between his beliefs and American praxis is a sign of his myopia. His mother was a realist motivated by the politics of want, resentment of her poverty and the frustration of her ambitions. If she hadn't been poor, Daniel suspects, she would never have become a communist. Between naive idealism and grim realism, the Isaacsons await the millennium of justice and retribution.

Daniel's mother, Rochelle, may have been a realist but her pessimism is merely the converse of her husband's dreamy

42

optimism: both are signs of an inability to make the necessary connections between desire and reality. Daniel notes:

> Her weaknesses were not as obvious to me as Paul's. If someone claims to deal with life so as to survive, you grant him soundness of character. But she was as unstable as he was. In her grim expectations. In her refusal to have illusions. In her cold, dogmatic rage. As if there were some profound missed thing in her life which she could never forget. Some betrayal of promise. (*BD*, p. 53)

Guilty of self-deception, both parents become accomplices in their own destruction. This illuminates one of Doctorow's themes: the compulsion of the American Left to implicate itself in its own martyrdom. As Daniel sees it, 'The world was arranging itself to suit my mother and father, like some mystical alignment of forces in the air; so that frictionless and in physical harmony, all bodies and objects were secreting the one sentiment that was their Passion, that would take them from me' (*BD*, p. 124). So we may say that the Isaacsons are co-conspirators along with the FBI and the Communist Party in their own immolation.

It is this complex legacy that all the children in the novel must learn to accept. When Daniel confronts Mindish's daughter Linda at the end of the novel he is forced to recognize the identity of their situations. 'For one moment I experienced the truth of the situation as an equitability of evil,' he says. 'I saw her as locked in her family truths as we were locked in ours' (*BD*, p. 291). In different ways the children are imprisoned in the past: the novel recounts their struggles to deal with the burden of parental sins and break the chain of inherited injustices.

In the characters of Daniel, his sister Susan, and Artie Sternlicht, the New Left radical who sounds like Jerry Rubin, Doctorow depicts the problematic inheritance bequeathed by the Old Left. For Sternlicht, the problem is easily resolved. The Old Left heritage must be rejected. 'You want to know what was wrong with the old American Communists?' he tells

Daniel. 'They were into the system. They wore ties. They held down jobs. They put people up for President. They thought politics is something you do at a meeting. When they got busted they called it tyranny. They were Russian tit suckers. Russia! Who's free in Russia? All the Russians want is steel up every-one's ass. Where's the Revolution in Russia?' In Sternlicht's view, the Old Left was simply part of the same system that must be destroyed. No wonder he concludes: 'The American Com-munist Party set the Left back fifty years. I think they worked for the FBI. That's the only explanation. They were conspirato-rial. They were invented by J. Edgar Hoover. They were his greatest invention' (*BD*, p. 166).

As Sternlicht sees it, revolution requires a total transfor-mation of consciousness and a complete rejection of history. A child of the new technology and the old romanticism, he wants to make a revolution of feelings in which the government will be overthrown with images. But Sternlicht's uncompromising position is as out of touch with the American reality as Paul Isaacson's. Like Paul, he underestimates the repressive power of the state and overestimates the revolutionary power of the individual. According to Sternlicht, society is a 'put-on' sus-tained by the inertia of authority which can be exposed as a simple illusion. Society may be a put-on but it still has the power to electrocute you, as Daniel, an authority on 'thermal pollution', knows from experience. Moreover, Sternlicht's own power is exaggerated, as he himself admits when he confesses that he is sick and has no energy. Finally, though he recognizes that the revolution has created too many martyrs already, he is still willing to be added to their number.

Susan stands in opposition to Sternlicht. She is imprisoned in the past, governed by the rage to preserve her parents' memory. Her obsession with her parents' execution is the driving force of her radicalism: the revolutionary foundation which she wishes to establish with her part of the inheritance has as its first objective the commemoration of their martyrdom. But, as Sternlicht remarks, the revolution has more martyrs than it needs. Thus Susan's obsession with the past effectively cuts her off from the other young radicals who wish to abolish history. Daniel realizes this when he gets her suicide note:

THEY'RE STILL FUCKING US. She didn't mean Paul and Rochelle. That's what I would have meant. What she meant was first everyone else and now the Left. The Isaacsons are nothing to the New Left. And if you can't make it with them who else is there? YOU GET THE PICTURE, GOODBYE, DANIEL. (*BD*, p. 169)

Susan's passion for the past and resentment of the present turn her inward to the point of madness. Like the mythical starfish whose five points are aimed inward towards the centre, she strives for a measure of harmony that is humanly impossible. Instead she achieves a degree of withdrawal that resembles death. 'Today Susan is a starfish,' Daniel tells us. 'Today she practices the silence of the starfish. There are few silences deeper than the silence of the starfish. There are not many degrees of life lower before there is no life' (*BD*, p. 223). Like her parents before her, Susan has lost the ability to make the connections between her desires and reality. 'My sister is dead,' Daniel concludes. 'She died of a failure of analysis' (*BD*, p. 317).

Finally, we may say that Susan dies of heart failure: the failure of the heart to keep itself intact in the face of the world's injustice. Her vulnerability to pain is finally too great. In her heartbroken response to life, she resembles the other women in her family. Daniel imagines them all as textbook examples: 'This is a medical textbook. The meaning of the picture is in the thin, diagrammatical arrow line, colored red, that runs from Grandma's breast through your mama's and into your sister's. The red line describes the progress of madness inherited through the heart' (*BD*, p. 83).

Susan's problem then is not that she keeps her feelings in but that she cannot keep the world out. Daniel's problem is the opposite: not that he cannot let his feelings out but that he refuses to let the world in. This is the basis of his rejection of his parents, his foster parents, his wife and even his son. It seems that he too suffers from a heart condition. Musing on the difficulties that medical science encounters in perfecting the heart transplant, he observes that 'Doctors still have a lot to learn about why we reject our hearts' (BD, p. 309). This is Daniel's problem: his inability to accept the inclinations of his heart, his compulsion to reject both his past and his present. Beginning in a state of rage, he is only released from his psychic alienation by the senile Mindish's ambiguous blessing. Finally, he is able to forgive his family, his enemy, even himself. After such acceptance he is again capable of action.

'In a world divided in two the radical is free to choose one side or the other. That's the radical choice.' Throughout the novel Daniel is urged to choose; in the words of the old radical song that Sternlicht sings to him: 'WHICH SIDE ARE YOU ON?' (BD, p. 170). Finally, he makes the radical choice but only after he has learnt to do it without rejecting his heart. In two climactic scenes – first in his confrontation with the state on the steps of the Pentagon and then in his meeting with Mindish in the heart of Disneyland – Daniel is finally liberated from his past by confronting and accepting it. 'Listen,' he tells his wife after he has been arrested at the Pentagon, 'It looks worse than it is. There was nothing to it. It is a lot easier to be a revolutionary nowadays then it used to be' (BD, p. 274). This is where Daniel's acceptance of his radical legacy is more complete than either Sternlicht's or Susan's. For Sternlicht, the past must be repudiated before the future can be redeemed. As he says, 'EVERYTHING THAT CAME BEFORE IS ALL THE SAME!' (BD, p. 151). His refusal of history is a sign of his weakness. For Susan, obsessed with her parents' execution, the present must be repudiated if the past is to be redeemed. Her refusal of reality is a symptom of her insanity. Finally, it is left to Daniel to connect history and reality by burying the past and bearing witness to it in the present. Released by Mindish's kiss, he can accept ambiguity without being paralysed. 'Of one thing we are sure,' he says. 'Everything is elusive. God is elusive. Revolutionary morality is elusive. Justice is elusive. Human character' (BD, p. 54).

Perhaps we can now make sense of the three endings that Doctorow has provided for his novel. In the first, Daniel returns to his parents' house only to discover that he is a stranger viewed with suspicion by the present poor black occupants. 'I would like to turn and ask the woman if I can come in the house and look around,' he says. 'But the children gather up the cards and go inside and their mother shuts the door. I will do nothing. It's their house now' (*BD*, p. 315). In the second, Daniel must bury his sister and, at the same time, relive his parents' funeral. In a moving scene, he has Kaddish, the Jewish prayer for the dead, said over the graves of both Susan and his parents. 'The funeral director waits impatiently beside his shiny hearse. But I encourage the prayermakers, and when one is through I tell him *again*, this time for my mother and father. Isaacson. Pinchas. Rachele. Susele. For all of them. I hold my wife's hand. And I think I am going to be able to cry.'

Having buried the dead, Daniel must now return to the present. 'For my third ending,' he writes, 'I had hoped to discuss some of the questions posed by this narrative. However, just a moment ago, while I was sitting here writing the last page, someone came through announcing that the library is closed.' It is 1968 and the student radicals are closing down Columbia University in protest against the Vietnam war. 'Close the book, man,' he is told, 'what's the matter with you, don't you know you're liberated?' This is finally what Daniel must do: close the book and re-enter the world. 'I have to smile,' he concludes. 'It has not been unexpected. I will walk out to the Sundial and see what's going down' (*BD*, p. 318).

Like Daniel, the reader is led back to the real world of social relations at the end of the novel. The multiplicity of endings suggests both the process of self-realization and the continuity of history. This idea of continuity is emphasized first in the title. Daniel makes explicit connections between his book and its biblical counterpart. He compares the Cold War climate, with its overtones of anti-Semitism, to the situation in ancient Babylon. Just as the king sentences Daniel's brothers to death in the fiery furnace, so the state condemns Daniel's parents to death in the electric chair. As survivors, both the biblical and the contemporary Daniel are haunted by nightmares they cannot interpret and thus thrown into spiritual crisis. 'I, Daniel, was grieved in my spirit in the midst of my body, and the vision of my head troubled me. . . . My cogitations much troubled me, and my countenance changed in me: but I kept the matter in my heart' (*BD*, p. 22).

The theme of continuity is repeated in the history of alienation in three generations of Daniel's family. Displaced from the *shtetl*, his grandmother goes mad in the New World when her family is destroyed and her children abandon the old language and traditions. Estranged from their Jewish roots, his parents choose American names and the secular millennialism of Marxism. Branded as the son of traitors, Daniel repudiates the family name along with its religion and politics. Yet there is also continuity in the generational revolt. His mother's 'politics was like Grandma's religion – some purchase on the future against the terrible life of the present' (*BD*, p. 53). His father 'could forswear his Jewish heritage and take for his own the perfectionist dream of heaven on earth, and in spite of that, or perhaps because of it, still consider himself a Jew' (*BD*, p. 134). Finally, Daniel also returns to the family tradition he has rejected by accepting the family name, religion and politics in the concluding scenes of burial and rebirth.

But Daniel's acceptance of his heritage is more than a family matter because Doctorow is describing something larger. 'I think that all writers in all nations operate as children do of families whom they love and hate and try to distinguish themselves from and somehow reform at the same time. And I would put a nation's artists in that category – as loving and tortured children' (*EC*, p. 57). In the novel, Daniel is that loving and tortured child, 'a little criminal of perception', driven by his conflicting emotions to accept his role as witness in dark times (*BD*, p. 44). No wonder, then, that he writes his book instead of his doctoral dissertation and that he names Edgar Allan Poe as our 'archetypel traitor' and 'Master subversive . . . who wore a hole into the parchment and let the darkness pour through' (*BD*, p. 193). *The Book of Daniel* is a dark book but it is irradiated by compassion. Like its biblical counterpart, it is an intense and complex song of lamentation both passionate and prophetic.

4

FICTION AND HISTORY

But in retrospect, I suppose (speaking of *Ragtime* and *The Book of Daniel*) there is some kind of disposition – and no more than that – to propose that all our radicals (and we've had an astonishing number of them) and our labor leaders and our Wobblies and our anarchists and so on, have really been intimate members of the family – black sheep, as it were, whom no one likes to talk about. And I suppose one could make a case for my disposition to suggest that they are indeed related, that they are part of the family, and that they've had an important effect on the rest of us. (*EC*, pp. 67–8)

The second climactic scene of *The Book of Daniel* takes place, appropriately enough, in Disneyland. The confrontation between Daniel and Mindish which involves an attempt to retrieve the past occurs in the place which has already abolished history. Under Daniel's analysis, Disneyland is revealed as a suitable symbol for the coming 'one-dimensional society' described by Herbert Marcuse. By a 'radical process of reduction' Disneyland eliminates the dialectical dimension of both literature and history in its 'cartoon' rendering of reality.

The life and life-style of slave-trading America on the Mississippi River in the 19th century is compressed into a technologically faithful steamboat ride of five or ten minutes on an HO-scale river. The intermediary between us and this actual historical experience, the writer Mark Twain, author of *Life on the Mississippi*, is now no more than the name of the boat. (*BD*, p. 304)

Furthermore, the one-dimensional nature of Disneyland is mirrored by the homogeneous character of its clientele. Just as its version of American history excludes minorities and deviant groups, so Daniel notices how few blacks, Mexicans, hippies and long-haired young people are permitted in Disneyland. Daniel is aware of the political implications in all this.

> What Disneyland proposes is a technique of abbreviated shorthand culture for the masses, a mindless thrill, like an electric shock, that insists at the same time on the recipient's rich psychic relation to his country's history and language and literature. In a forthcoming time of highly governed masses in an overpopulated world, this technique may be extremely useful both as a substitute for education and, eventually, as a substitute for experience. (*BD*, p. 305)

This Disneyland view of American reality is the starting point of Doctorow's next novel, *Ragtime*, which returns us to the beginning of this century. As the narrator tells us on the first page:

> Patriotism was a reliable sentiment in the early 1900's. Teddy Roosevelt was President. The population customarily gathered in great numbers either out of doors for parades, public concerts, fish fries, political picnics, social outings, or indoors in meeting halls, vaudeville theatres, operas, ballrooms. There seemed to be no entertainment that did not involve great swarms of people. Trains and steamers and trolleys moved them from one place to another. That was the style, that was the way people lived. Women were stouter then. They visited the fleet carrying white parasols. Everyone wore white in the summer. Tennis racquets were hefty and the racquet faces elliptical. There was a lot of sexual fainting. There were no Negroes. There were no immigrants. (*R*, pp. 3–4)

'That was the style, that was the way people lived.' From the beginning, the cool, detached, slightly ironic narrative voice, so different from Daniel's intense, involving, complex rhetoric, distances us from the events of *Ragtime* as it rewrites American history. *Ragtime* begins with the conventional view of the turn of the century as an age of innocence but then reveals the social and economic conflicts that remained barely suppressed beneath the surface. 'Apparently there *were* Negroes. There *were* immigrants' (R, p. 5). If American history has traditionally been written from the vantage point of the dominant culture, then in *Ragtime* Doctorow rewrites it 'from the bottom up'.

Doctorow's revisioning of American history bears comparison with that of John Dos Passos and, indeed, several critics have drawn attention to the similarities between *Ragtime* and *U.S.A.* John Seelye has observed:

> What Doctorow has done is to take the materials of John Dos Passos' *U.S.A.* – a sequential series of fictional, biographical and historical episodes – and place them in a compactor, reducing the bulk and hopelessly blurring the edges of definition. And yet the result is an artifact which retains the specific gravity of Dos Passos' classic, being a massively cynical indictment of capitalist, racist, violent, crude, crass and impotently middle-class America.[29]

But despite these striking resemblances, *Ragtime* is not modelled on *U.S.A.* In fact, as Barbara Foley has pointed out, their views of history are opposite.[30] For Dos Passos, history has an objective order which provides the structure of his fiction. For Doctorow, on the other hand, objective history is a chimera. 'There is no history except as it is composed,' he has written. 'That is why history has to be written and rewritten from one generation to another. The act of composition never ends' (EC, p. 24). Similarly, in *Ragtime* it is evident to the little boy who will grow up to write the narrative that 'the world composed and recomposed itself in an endless process of dissatisfaction' (R, p. 135).

In *U.S.A.* history and fiction are treated as distinct entities and separated into discrete compartments of narrative, newsreel, biography and autobiography. Dos Passos is scrupulous in his historical research to the point where he was actually accused of plagiarism in one of his biographies. History in *U.S.A.* is highly interpreted but it is never invented: indeed,

Dos Passos's faith in an objective order of reality led him to portray his biographical figures as the agents of history and his fictional figures as its victims. On the other hand, *Ragtime* is shaped by the conflation of history and fiction where the boundary line between the two seems to disappear. Not only does Doctorow invent incidents in the lives of his historical personages but his 'real' and 'imagined' characters meet and mingle promiscuously on an equal footing, both victims and agents of their own projections of history. In Doctorow's view, 'history is a kind of fiction in which we live and hope to survive, and fiction is a kind of speculative history, perhaps a superhistory, by which the available data for the composition is seen to be greater and more various in its sources than the historian supposes' (*EC*, p. 25).

The freedom that Doctorow achieves by this strategy is quite dazzling. The fictional characters like Coalhouse Walker take on a certain gravity as they enter history while the representative figures of the age are both illuminated and demythologized, as in Freud's boat trip through the Tunnel of Love with Jung. Even the great villains of an era of rapacious capitalism are radically altered. Compare, for instance, Dos Passos's dour picture of the House of Morgan with Doctorow's witty portrait of J. P. Morgan. In *Ragtime*, the irresistible engine of monopoly capitalism is driven by a group of quite ordinary men who do not comprehend the forces they have unleashed. When Morgan invites the dozen most powerful men in America to a 'historic' dinner party he finds them to be less prepossessing than he had imagined.

> He was hoping the collected energy of their minds might buckle the walls of his home. Rockefeller startled him with the news that he was chronically constipated and did a lot of his thinking on his toilet. Carnegie dozed over his brandy. Harriman uttered inanities. Gathered in this one room the business elite could think of nothing to say. (*R*, p. 160)

Nevertheless, Morgan hands out laurel wreaths and has a photograph taken of the 'historic' occasion.[31]

Here, as elsewhere in the novel, appearance belies reality. In Doctorow's hands, history demystified becomes a ragbag of accidents (the Archduke is assassinated when his chauffeur takes a wrong turn); coincidences (both Tateh and Henry Ford deal with the same Franklin Novelty Company); parallels (Coalhouse Walker meets Booker T. Washington in the same place that J. P. Morgan entertained Henry Ford); and mis-understandings (the Archduke congratulates Houdini on the invention of the aeroplane). To impose order on chaos requires an imaginative act. Like Daniel, the little boy must learn to make connections; like Doctorow, he is never surprised by contingency. Yet reality remains as elusive as the precise location of the North Pole. Admiral Peary 'couldn't find the exact place to say this spot, here, is the North Pole. Never-theless there was no question that they were there' (R, p. 90). The artist's perception remains a matter of shifting per-spectives as Theodore Dreiser demonstrates when he tries to properly align his chair. 'Throughout the night Dreiser turned his chair in circles seeking the proper alignment' (R, p. 30).

The kaleidoscopic quality of Ragtime underscores the pro-tean nature of reality, like the stories from Ovid that the boy hears from his grandfather. Some critics have seen in this interplay of forces a pattern of repetition which suggests a cyclical view of history. 'Little has changed despite all that has occurred in Ragtime,' argued Arthur Saltzman; 'the novel opens with Father making a living from patriotism, and the market still exists when the novel's frame is completed years later' (EC, p. 99). True enough. But this fails to take into account the fundamental changes that occur in the course of the novel. On the personal level, Ragtime begins by chronicling the lives of three 'families' – WASP, immigrant and black – whose existences are entirely segregated. By the end of the book these three families have become one. On the public level, Ragtime describes the transformation of American society from small-town WASP homogeneity to big-city ethnic hetero-geneity. The immigrants and Negroes who were excluded from

American reality at the beginning of the novel have by the end become part of the family.

Furthermore, the generational conflicts in the novel suggest shifting political perspectives. Just as Younger Brother is more radical than Father, so Coalhouse Walker is less revolutionary than his younger followers. Thus Father comes to the conclusion that he and Coalhouse are true contemporaries who share similar beliefs in dignity, property and justice. 'But the people following him were not. They were another generation. They were not human. Father shuddered. They were monstrous! Their cause had recomposed their minds. They would kick at the world's supports. Start an army! They were nothing more than filthy revolutionaries' (*R*, p. 337).

The view of history presented here is more dialectical than cyclical. At times, particularly in the story of Coalhouse Walker, Doctorow's treatment of history is deliberately anachronistic in the way it reshapes the past to parallel the present. Walker's meeting with Booker T. Washington, for instance, echoes the contemporary debate between integrationists and black separatists. Similarly, Henry Ford is described as the father of mass society and Evelyn Nesbit is depicted as the first sex goddess of mass culture. The revolutionary implications of Evelyn's image are recognized both by the businessmen who manufacture it and by the radicals who challenge it. 'I am often asked the question How can the masses permit themselves to be exploited by the few,' Emma Goldman explains to Evelyn. 'The answer is By being persuaded to identify with them. Carrying his newspaper with your picture the laborer goes home to his wife, an exhausted workhorse with the veins standing out in her legs, and he dreams not of justice but of being rich' (*R*, p. 96).

In its mixture of fact and fiction, *Ragtime* is closer to romance than to the conventions of traditional history fiction. Though it is the witty historical inventions which have received the most attention, Doctorow was as concerned with the stylistic problems of his narrative.

In *Ragtime* it was the historical imagery and the mock-historical tone which most interested me. And the idea of composition at a fixed narrative distance to the subject, neither as remote as history writing – which is very, very distant from what is being described – nor as close as modern fiction, which is very intimate with the subject. I was aiming for the narrative distance of the historical chronicle that you find, for instance, in Kleist who, of course, was very important in the composition of that book. (*EC*, p. 39)

Indeed, *Ragtime* owes more to Heinrich von Kleist's 'Michael Kohlhaas' than to Dos Passos's *U.S.A.* Kleist's tale, itself based on a historical chronicle, recounts the efforts of an honest and respected horse dealer to obtain justice from the corrupt feudal society he had accepted. 'I had always wanted to rework the circumstances of Kleist's story,' observed Doctorow. 'I felt the premise was obviously relevant, appropriate – the idea of a man who cannot find justice from a society that claims to be just' (*EC*, p. 44). Doctorow's translation into an American cultural idiom is both apt and inventive. Michael Kohlhaas becomes Coalhouse Walker and Kohlhaas's disputed horses are transformed into Coalhouse's ruined car. Even Kohlhaas's fateful interview with Martin Luther is repeated in Coalhouse's meeting with Booker T. Washington. Finally, there is a sly hint of acknowledgement when Coalhouse uses a silver tankard from J. P. Morgan's collection that had once belonged to Frederick, the elector of Saxony, to communicate with the police.

But the parallels which Doctorow wishes to exploit are more than merely formal. Both Kohlhaas and Coalhouse live in societies whose fragile surface order belies a fundamental instability. The protagonists' desperate actions, predicated upon their belief in the values their societies profess, reveal not simply the hypocrisy of the social order but its vulnerability in a time of profound social transformation. According to John Seelye, 'Michael Kohlhaas' describes the clash over the rights of property between the old landed and new monied classes which defined the transformation of Europe during the Renaissance. Similarly, *Ragtime* depicts the growing class conflict which characterized the era of the emerging modern American state where the belief in the sacredness of property took precedence over the commitment to the principle of equality before the law. Thus both Kohlhaas and Coalhouse become victims of their faith in a social system which is revealed to be based upon power and not justice. As Kleist describes Kohlhaas, 'the world would have had cause to revere his memory, had he not pursued one of his virtues to excess. But his sense of justice made him a robber and a murderer.'[32] Similarly, Doctorow describes how Coalhouse Walker's pursuit of justice is transformed into an implacable desire for vengeance. 'Or is injustice once suffered, a mirror universe, with laws of logic and principles of reason the opposite of civilization's?' (*R*, p. 311).

Yet Doctorow's adaptation has an added dimension. First, there is the intractable element of racism in American society which makes a normal life impossible for the protagonist despite all his efforts. Coalhouse Walker's problems begin with his refusal to accept his assigned social role. 'Walker didn't act or talk like a colored man. He seemed to be able to transform the customary deferences practised by his race so that they reflected to his own dignity rather than the recipient's' (*R*, p. 186). Coalhouse's ignorance of his racial identity is more calculated than innocent. He knows that possession of a car will be a provocation for many white people, especially members of the working class who envy his achievement. But the racism he experiences is an integral part of a class system in which the lower orders identify with their oppressors and maintain their precarious position on the slippery ladder of success by oppressing those beneath them. 'By what other standard could the craven and miserable Willie Conklin, a bigot so ordinary as to be like all men, become Pierpont Morgan, the most important individual of his time?' (*R*, p. 311).

Second, Doctorow transforms Kleist's horse dealer into a

modern artist: Coalhouse Walker's ragtime piano provides the central metaphor of the novel. 'The pianist sat stiffly at the keyboard, his long hands with their pink nails seemingly with no effort producing the clusters of syncopating chords and the thumping octaves' (*R*, p. 183). The musical image of 'syncopating chords' playing against 'thumping octaves' suggests the dialectical relationship in *Ragtime* between fiction and fact, individual will and historical necessity, the organic vision of community expressed by Emma Goldman and the mechanical view of corporate society created by Henry Ford. But ragtime is an appropriate image for the creative act itself. As Coalhouse plays Scott Joplin's 'Wall Street Rag' the little boy is transported to a world elsewhere. 'Small clear chords hung in the air like flowers. The melodies were like bouquets. There seemed to be no other possibilities for life than those delineated by the music' (*R*, p. 183).

But Coalhouse Walker is not the only proletarian artist in the novel. Both Houdini and Tateh also come from the working class and rise by creating new cultural forms. Houdini is a headliner in vaudeville, a forerunner of the superstars of the electronic media. But though he dedicates himself to the American ideal of self-perfection, he realizes that he can never escape his working-class origins. And though his escape acts become more sensational, he knows that they are merely escapist entertainments divorced from the real world where history is made. Houdini's problem is that he could never make the connection between art and life. Thus he 'never developed what we think of as a political consciousness. He could not reason from his own hurt feelings. To the end he would be almost totally unaware of the design of his career, the great map of revolution laid out by his life' (*R*, pp. 38–9). This is in contrast to Coalhouse Walker who is compelled by his colour to make the appropriate connections himself. When Emma Goldman is asked about her influence on the ragtime pianist-turned-terrorist, she responds: 'Wealth is the oppressor. Coalhouse Walker did not need Red Emma to learn that. He only needed to suffer' (*R*, p. 322).

More problematical is the story of Tateh, the silhouette artist who becomes a pioneer movie-maker. He begins as a socialist but his bitter experience of poverty and class oppression destroys his faith in revolutionary change. 'From this moment, perhaps, Tateh began to conceive of his life as separate from the fate of the working class' (*R*, p. 149). Whereas Coalhouse must give up the piano and become a terrorist, Tateh makes his escape by becoming a commercial artist and pointing 'his life along the lines of flow of American energy. Workers could strike and die but in the streets of cities an entrepreneur could cook sweet potatoes in a bucket of hot coals and sell them for a penny or two. A smiling hurdy-gurdy man could fill his cup' (*R*, p. 153). Tateh compromises in ways that Coalhouse cannot. He not only embraces the American dream as a way of erasing the past but he exploits the myth of success in the popular entertainment he now creates. Like a figure out of Horatio Alger, he creates a new existence as Baron Ashkenazy, a truly self-made man. 'His whole personality had turned outward and he had become a voluble and energetic man full of the future. He felt he deserved his happiness. He'd constructed it without help' (*R*, pp. 299–300). Yet Tateh's success has its costs in his loss of personal identity and though he has con-sciously betrayed his convictions he has not completely surren-dered his beliefs. His final vision of transforming his new interracial family experience into a series of *Our Gang* com-edies is both a touching reminder of his lost idealism and an ironic example of his corrupted sensibility.

If ragtime and movies are the controlling images of art in the novel it is because both are formally appropriate and quin-tessentially American. Whereas in Europe high and popular culture are strictly segregated and the influences are legitimized from the top down, in America the two cultures are intertwined and the distinctively American impulses move from the bottom up. Ragtime and motion pictures, vaudeville and baseball were all nourished by contributors from the lowly group of immi-grants and blacks. For Doctorow, the genius of American culture lies in its popular roots which flourish in the rich soil of ordinary life. Thus architects like Stanford White and collectors like J. P. Morgan, with their custodial view of culture, are really the 'alien' figures since they simply wish to impose European cultural standards on the conditions of American life. But in describing the resistance to the wholesale appropriation of European high culture, Doctorow is aware of the difference between an organic and creative popular culture and a mechanical and manufactured mass culture. As he observes about Houdini: 'Today, nearly fifty years since his death, the audience for escapes is even larger' (R, p. 8).

Interestingly enough, the publication of Ragtime illustrated some of Doctorow's ideas about the fluidity of American culture. Not only was the novel a critical success but it became a media event. Ragtime won the first National Book Critics Circle Award for fiction and was the best-selling novel of the year, even outstripping Jaws. In the first year of its publication, nearly a quarter of a million hardback copies were sold in the United States alone. Less than a year later, almost three million copies of the paperback edition had been printed. Rarely, if ever, had a serious novel entered the dizzying world of mass culture with such a splash. Kathy Piehl has chronicled the advertising campaigns launched by Random House and Bantam Books to make Ragtime a household word.[33] But public relations alone cannot account for the tremendous popularity that the novel enjoyed. Rather its fusion of 'highbrow' and 'popular' elements and its blend of 'revisionist' history and wry cynicism about national myths caught the imagination of post-Watergate America in much the same way as Robert Altman's contemporaneous film, Nashville. Ironically, the warm reception in America led British reviewers to treat the novel with a greater degree of scepticism. Yet the extraordinary success of Ragtime established Doctorow as a major figure in contemporary American letters.

Like his first two novels, Ragtime explores elements of popular culture. Like The Book of Daniel, it revises our understanding of modern history. Just as he celebrates those disreputable cultural forms that are distinctly American, so he commemorates those despised ethnic groups that have hitherto been excluded from American history. In the climactic scene of *U.S.A.*, Dos Passos hailed the martyred anarchists Sacco and Vanzetti as the true heirs to the American pioneer spirit. In *Ragtime*, Doctorow goes a step further to suggest how the American character has been profoundly affected by its foreign and alienated elements. As in his earlier fiction, Doctorow uses the family as a symbol of our connectedness even in the midst of our great differences.

> But in retrospect, I suppose ... there is some kind of disposition ... to propose that all our radicals (and we've had an astonishing number of them) ... have really been intimate members of the family – black sheep, as it were, whom no one likes to talk about. And I suppose one could make a case for my disposition to suggest that they are indeed related, that they are part of the family, and that they've had an important effect on the rest of us. (*EC*, pp. 67–8)

Ragtime is not only proof of the proposition but a splendid example of how fiction can revise our understanding of history, of how imagination can reclaim the world of facts. 'If you ask me whether some things in the book "really" happened,' Doctorow affirms, 'I can only say, "They have now."'[34]

5

FICTION AND
THE AMERICAN DREAM

I was driving through the Adirondacks a couple of years ago.
I found myself incredibly responsive to everything I saw and
heard and smelled. The Adirondacks are very beautiful – but
more than that, a palpably mysterious wilderness, a place
full of dark secrets, history rotting in the forests. At least that
was my sense of things. I saw a road sign: 'Loon Lake.'
Everything I felt came to a point in those words. I liked their
sound. I imagined a private railroad train going through the
forest. The train was taking a party of gangsters to the
mountain retreat of a powerful man of great wealth. So there
it was: A feeling for a place, an image or two, and I was off in
pursuit of my book. (*EC*, p. 40)

After the extraordinary popular and critical success of *Ragtime*, Doctorow first turned away from fiction to follow other
creative pursuits. He became involved in the film project for
Ragtime and even appeared in Robert Altman's movie version
of *Buffalo Bill and the Indians* (he can be seen in the Gala scene
standing, appropriately enough, to the left of President Cleveland). Then he turned to drama and wrote *Drinks Before
Dinner* which was produced at the New York Shakespeare
Festival's Public Theater in 1978. Yet all this activity had a
direct bearing on his next novel, *Loon Lake*.

Drinks Before Dinner is an unusual play for several reasons.
First of all, its point of departure is linguistic, not ideological.
According to Doctorow, the play did not originate in a story or
an idea, as is usually the case, but in a particular mode of
speech. 'It was not until I had the sound of it in my ear that I
thought about saying something. The language preceded the
intention.' This emphasis on language is not so unusual for a

writer whose fiction has been determined by the discovery of an appropriate narrative voice for each work. 'Writers live in language, and their seriousness of purpose is not compromised nor their convictions threatened if they acknowledge that the subject of any given work may be a contingency of song' (*DD*, p. ix).

Moreover, *Drinks Before Dinner* is not a conventional drama which focuses upon the development of character. Instead, as Doctorow argued, 'The idea of character as we normally celebrate it on the American stage is what this play seems to question' (*DD*, pp. xi–xii). The result is a play that is intentionally non-dramatic, involving actors who are not really characters speaking lines that approximate the rhetorical mode of Gertrude Stein and Mao Tse-tung. Though 'the real suspense is to see how much diffuse complaint the artist can get away with before the occasion loses power', the intention and method of the play are neither absurdist nor surreal (*DD*, p. xix). *Drinks Before Dinner* is a variation on conventional drawing-room drama in which an apparently normal and respectable man pulls a gun at a dinner party and 'hijacks' a living room full of people and compels them to confront the desperate vulnerability of contemporary life. The hijacker is neither a 'criminal psychopath' nor a 'revolutionary' but a 'moral hysteric' who bears some resemblance to the ancient prophets in his apocalyptic vision (*DD*, p. xvii). Interestingly enough, his name, like Doctorow's, is Edgar. For Edgar, the living room becomes a space cleared of the falsehoods and self-deceptions that obscure reality: 'a new territory, a region of light in which the truth of our situation is acknowledged. That is revolutionary!' (*DD*, p. 52). But by the end of the evening Edgar is disarmed of his gun and his illusions, and the dinner party goes on as planned. 'Nevertheless,' suggested Doctorow, 'a community of perception has been formed. Condemned, renounced and alone – dinner about to be served' (*DD*, p. xviii).

Drinks Before Dinner is unusual in Doctorow's *oeuvre* because its form is dramatic, its setting contemporary and its cast of characters exclusively middle class. Indeed, the play appears to traffic in generalizations about the anxieties underlying bourgeois affluence: urban decay, environmental pollution, nuclear holocaust, the corruption of political and cultural life. The play's originality lies not in these statements but in the way the speeches reveal the social situation. In Doctorow's words:

> It is a play turned inside out. It displays human beings not filled in with the colors and textures of their individual peculiarity, but delineated from the outlines provided by the things that shape them, their technology, their failing rituals and faltering institutions, their platitudinous ideas and common fears. They are invisible presences, these people, ghosts, shown only as a space in their surroundings. (*DD*, p. xvi)

In *Drinks Before Dinner*, characters do not express ideas, ideas express character.

At first glance, there would appear to be little to connect Doctorow's drama of contemporary affluence with his novel of the Depression years, *Loon Lake*. But, in fact, they have much in common. Both began as experiments with language: the play as discursive prose that turned out to be a monologue, the novel as blank verse that became a narrative device. Furthermore, the monologist, Edgar, and the versifier, Warren Penfield, are remarkably similar: like Edgar, Penfield is an anguished witness, more interested in self-dramatization than in social action or even personal revenge. Finally, the idea of a character shaped from the outside rather than from the inside, of an actor totally determined by his role, is central to both the play and the novel. Their shared preoccupation is with 'the corruption of human identity'. Their common theme is the emptiness of American life.

If Doctorow took his concern for language from the theatre, he borrowed his narrative techniques from film. As he once explained, what we've learned from film is quite explicit. We've learned that we don't have to explain things. We don't have to explain how our man can be in the bedroom one moment and walking in the street the next. How he can be twenty years old one moment and eighty years old a moment later. We've learned that if we can just make the book happen, the reader can take care of himself. (*EC*, p. 41)

Already in *The Book of Daniel* Doctorow began to break up his narrative by jumping back and forth in time and even changing point of view. But in *Loon Lake* the principle of discontinuity is taken one step further. Here we encounter a number of narrative voices, with characters speaking in both first and third person, shifting suddenly in time and space. The novel moves swiftly, changing voice or scene often, and filling the necessary exposition with a computer printout, a device which resembles the movie montage in its ability to provide information in shorthand. Thus the narrative is both complex and compressed: 'It is the account in helpless linear translation of the unending love of our simultaneous but disynchronous lives' (*LL*, p. 291).

Corruption and emptiness are evident in the setting which gives the novel its title. Loon Lake is the idyllic domain of a wealthy capitalist named F. W. Bennett, a private empire carved out of the American landscape. In a computer printout Doctorow swiftly traces the corruption of Loon Lake from its simple exploitation by trappers and hunters to its total appropriation by Bennett. In Doctorow's version of capitalist development, artists play a significant role as they are the first to assign a value to nature beyond the utilitarian:

But one summer after the May flies painters and poets arrived who paid money to sit in guide boats and to stand momentously above the gorges of rushing streams. The artists and poets patrons seeking and hearing their reports bought vast tracts of the Adirondacks very cheaply and began to build elaborate camps there thus inventing the wilderness as luxury. (*LL*, p. 49)

The pattern of transformation of nature from landscape to commodity was, of course, explored in *Welcome to Hard Times*. But whereas the Western landscape was characterized as blank and barren, Loon Lake is described as cold and remote, like its owner. Traditionally, the lake in American literature has symbolized the inviolable purity of nature, as in Cooper's Lake Glimmerglass and Thoreau's Walden. But in Doctorow's anti-romantic vision – which Diane Johnson has termed 'urban romantic'[35] – Loon Lake is icy and insular: the perfect objective correlative of capitalism in which the pursuit of wealth is motivated by the desire for complete isolation.

The idea of absolute freedom totally insulated from accountability is mirrored in the remoteness of Loon Lake from the outside world of the Depression while the image of the predatory loon becomes a metaphor for the activities of the characters. When Joe, the picaresque hero of the novel, runs away from the circus he escapes 'into the woods as to another world' (*LL*, p. 151). But soon he discovers that there is an essential connection between the realms of society and wilderness:

> I looked back up the hill to the house and felt the imposition of an enormous will on the natural planet. Stillness and peace, not the sound of a car or a horn or even a human voice, and I felt Loon Lake in its isolation, the bought wilderness, and speculated what I would do if I had the money. Would I purchase isolation, as this man had? Was that what money was for, to put a distance of fifty thousand acres of mountain terrain between you and the boondocks of the world?
>
> The man made automobile bodies, and they were for connection, cars were democracy we had been told.
>
> The wind rose in a sudden gust about my ears, and as I looked back to the lake, a loon was coming in like a roller coaster. He hit the water and skidded for thirty yards, sending up a great spray, and when the water settled he was gone. I couldn't see him, I thought the fucker had drowned. But up he popped, shaking and mauling a fat fish. And when

the fish was polished off, I heard a weird maniac cry coming off the water, and echoing off the hills. (*LL*, pp. 82–3)

Loon Lake resonates with certain indelible images from the accumulated American culture. The descriptions of the lake recall not only the setting of Thoreau's retreat in *Walden* but the scene of Clyde Griffiths' crime in *An American Tragedy*. The representation of Bennett's estate suggests Fitzgerald's 'Diamond as Big as the Ritz' and the portrayal of the poor young hero doggedly pursuing his dream girl echoes, of course, *The Great Gatsby*. But the other side of the novel, the description of Depression-ridden America wracked by class oppression and labour strife, also draws on the rich popular culture of the 1930s, from the gangster film to Frank Capra's comedies, from the strike novel to James M. Cain's melodramas. *Loon Lake* is very much a book about the 1930s but, as Doctorow has suggested, it is 'about our idea of the Thirties' (*I*).

In Doctorow's version, the dream of success thrives in the popular imagination even in the midst of the Great Depression. The unequal halves of American society exist side by side but the rich are insulated from the sight of poverty around them while the poor are exposed to the images of wealth to which they aspire. Just as the servants at Loon Lake identify with their employer so poor boys like Joe and Penfield are attracted to the signs of power and culture represented by Bennett. Richard King has suggested that *Loon Lake* 'might be subtitled "Why there is no Socialism in America." For what [Doctorow] presents us with is the immensely seductive power of the bourgeoisie and its ability to "buy" everyone off.' Thus the novel 'charts the triumph of energy over ideology, status over solidarity.'[36]

Doctorow's central metaphor for capitalist society is Sim Hearn's broken-down carnival. When Joe joins the circus he first learns 'how money was made from the poor. They drifted in, appearing starved and sucked dry, but holding in their palms the nickels and dimes that would give them a view of Wolf Woman, Lizard Man, the Living Oyster, the Fingerling

Family and in fact the whole Hearn Bros. bestiary of human virtue and excellence' (*LL*, p. 15). From the start, Joe identifies with the con men instead of their marks. Yet he also understands the similarity between the circus people and their victims. Though they appear exotic, the carney families are characterized by their ordinariness. 'The freaks read the papers and talked about Roosevelt, just like everyone else in the country' (*LL*, p. 18).

In fact, the carnival is simply a distorted mirror image of the normal society in which the wised-up freaks are working stiffs who are exploited like everyone else. 'They were mostly immigrants, after all – the same people but with a twist who worked for pennies in the sawmills or stood on the bread lines' (*LL*, p. 145). Indeed the most terrifying image of exploitation in the novel is not the mine disaster or the assembly line but the gang rape of the Fat Lady. In his total absorption with the pursuit of profit, the carnival-owner is simply another calculating entrepreneur and cold-eyed employer.

The resemblance between the carnival and Loon Lake is clear. Hearn is a distorted (or demystified) version of Bennett just as his wife Magda, a crippled trapeze artist, is a fallen version of Lucinda Bennett, a famous aviatrix. In his circus realm, Hearn is also an absolute ruler like the master of Loon Lake or the emperor of Japan. When Joe has an affair with Magda he is bothered that Hearn remains unperturbed. 'But his distance from me was unchanged and his peculiar authority maintained itself in my mind. It was as if no matter what I did to his wife I could never break through that supreme indifference' (*LL*, p. 144). Similarly, Joe's relationship with Bennett is undisturbed by the fact that he has run off with Bennett's mistress, Clara. For what characterizes Hearn and Bennett is their emotional aloofness. What they share is an essential impersonality. Their outstanding quality is their hollowness.

Yet Doctorow is too honest and clever a novelist to make his antagonist simply evil. Bennett and the capitalism he represents must be attractive for the novel to work. 'He's a very capable human being. Quite charming at times,' Penfield tells Joe. 'The mistake most people make is to jump to conclusions before they even meet him' (*LL*, p. 78). Joe, too, is attracted to the man's impersonal power, which manifests itself in a manic energy and a sense of complete personal freedom. Capable of both generosity and cruelty, Bennett explains to Joe his philosophy which is a curious blend of Existentialism and Social Darwinism:

> 'Every kind of life has its demands, its tests. Can I do this? Can I live with the consequences of what I'm doing? If you can't answer yes, you're in a life that's too much for you. Then you drop down a notch. If you can't steal and you can't sap someone on the head when you have to, you can join the line at the flophouse. You get on the bread line. If you can't muscle your way into the bread line, you sit at the curb and hold out your hand. You're a beggar. If you can't whine and wheedle and beg your cup of coffee, if you can't take the billy on the bottoms of your feet – why, I say be a poet.' (*LL*, p. 125)

The best that such a system can produce is embodied in Lucinda Bennett, whose soaring accomplishments symbolize life's transcendent possibilities. Flight is, after all, the aspiration of each of the characters: a solitary activity which defies the burden of gravity. 'I told her she liked the sky because it was clean,' Bennett observes of his wife. 'I never flew with her because I sensed it was her realm.' But Lucinda's desire for transcendence involves a fundamental self-denial. 'If it were possible for Lucinda to exist without a body she would have chosen to. Her body was of no interest to her' (*LL*, p. 287).

Like Loon Lake itself, Lucinda is insulated from the desires and corruptions of a fallen world. Yet elsewhere in the novel the connection between sexual and economic exploitation is made explicit. In this sense, Clara and the Fat Lady provide the same function at Loon Lake and the carnival respectively. In a provocative essay, David S. Gross has argued that Doctorow's fiction illustrates the relationship between money, power and excrement in capitalist society.[37] This is certainly true of *Loon Lake* where both the Fat Lady's gang rape and Magda's violation by Joe are connected with dirt and money, where both Penfield and Joe are transfixed by memories of little girls urinating, where Bennett's union-busting colleague is a gangster named Tommy Crapo, and where Bennett himself is compared to 'an emperor, a maniac force in pantaloons and silk slippers and lacquered headdress dispensing like treasure pieces of his stool' (*LL*, p. 293). Gross based his argument on Norman O. Brown's analysis of 'Filthy Lucre' in *Life Against Death*. According to Brown, the connection between wealth and anality in capitalist society reveals that the concept of money is rooted in feelings of guilt. For Doctorow, as for Brown, capitalism is based on repression.

Yet Doctorow's treatment of capitalism is complex in its weighing of virtues and vices. Private profit and public service, self-expression and self-denial, competition and co-operation vie with each other in a system which celebrates abundance but creates scarcity. Like John D. Rockefeller senior, Bennett is a robber baron who is both predator and philanthropist, a public figure who might steal millions and then give away dimes on the street. In a wickedly ironic passage, Doctorow balances the benefits and evils of capitalism, condemning its destructiveness while acknowledging its attractiveness:

> The benefits of such a system while occasionally random and unpredictable with periods of undeniable stress and misery depression starvation and degradation are inevitably distributed to a greater and greater percentage of the population. The periods of economic stability also ensure a greater degree of popular political freedom and among the industrial Western democracies today despite occasional suppression of free speech quashing of dissent corruption of public officials and despite the tendency of legislation to serve the interests of the ruling business oligarchy the poisoning of the air water the chemical adulteration of food the obscene development of hideous weaponry the increased costs of

simple survival the waste of human resources the ruin of cities the servitude of backward foreign populations, the standards of life under capitalism by any criterion are far greater than under state socialism in whatever forms it is found British Swedish Cuban Soviet or Chinese. (*LL*, pp. 184–5)

But *Loon Lake* is not simply a meditation on the power of American myths, it is also a commentary on the fate of American culture. In the 1930s, the radical discussion of culture focused on the new phenomenon of the proletarian novel. With the apparent failure of capitalism and the rising awareness of economic inequalities, intellectuals and artists on the Left hoped for the flowering of a new class-consciousness. Mike Gold, the nearest that America had to a cultural commissar, called for a new proletarian literature. In the pages of his magazine *The New Masses* he wanted to print the pure but crude expressions of the hitherto 'silent' working class: diaries of chambermaids, letters from hoboes, the poetry of steel workers, and stories about strikes, prisons or factories. At last, America would have a literature which dealt with the 'real' life of most of its citizens.

In the event, *The New Masses* printed little literature of lasting value before the radical concern for class-consciousness gave way to activity on behalf of a united front against fascism. It seemed impossible to challenge the dominant image of American life projected in the mass media. But even the most accomplished proletarian fiction of the period revealed a deep ambivalence about the reality of working-class solidarity. What novels as different as James T. Farrell's *Studs Lonigan*, Henry Roth's *Call It Sleep* and Richard Wright's *Native Son* shared, aside from impeccable proletarian credentials, was the conviction that racial, religious and ethnic identity was stronger in the United States than class solidarity. Thus rather than prove the existence of a strong working-class culture, the best proletarian fiction actually called into question the existence of class-consciousness.

In *Loon Lake* the major young characters – Penfield, Joe and Clara – are children of the working class in flight from their origins. In renouncing their respective familial legacies they all reject the ideal of class solidarity for the ideal of individual realization. Penfield's father wants Warren to work in the mines so that he will understand the sources of the old man's rage. He wants his son to grow up to be a great union organizer in order to justify his own frustrated life. But Warren's desire is, quite understandably, to escape the tawdry circumstances of his parents' existence. Rather than change reality by action he wishes to transform it by an act of imagination. Thus poetry becomes for Warren a way of organizing reality and transcending it as well.

Penfield's divided loyalties are tested in the 1919 Seattle General Strike, a unique occurrence in American history. As he walks through the orderly streets, he is excited by the prospect of the city being run by its ordinary working people. But when he tries to convey his sense of elation to his landlady, a staunch individualist, he is defeated by her scepticism towards the idea that institutions can be changed without a corresponding transformation of consciousness. Like Tateh at the Lawrence mill strike, Penfield lacks faith in the utopian possibilities of collective action. He is forced to admit that a revolution will be as imperfect as the men who make it. He runs away to Japan and enters a Zen monastery where he continues his search for inner revelation. His life takes on the pattern of flight that will lead him to his final destination, Loon Lake. 'The field of his accomplishment was his own private being, the grandness and depth of his failed affections' (*LL*, p. 111).

Like Penfield, Joe and Clara are also in flight from the deadening hand of their family background. Significantly enough, Clara's father is a mortician while Joe's joyless parents lead a desiccated existence which resembles a living death. In a neighbourhood where only the maniacs appear vital, rebellion and resistance are signs of life. Joe grows up in conscious opposition to this dreary working-class culture, stealing what he needs and hunting girls like prey. Clearly, the fittest to survive in that world are those who, like Joe, develop their predatory instincts: they look for trouble and are keen for life. Inevitably Joe leaves home, he joins the circus, and his life becomes 'a picaresque of other men's money and other men's women' (*LL*, p. 272). Thus Joe's journey is the mirror image of Penfield's: he joins the carnival where he encounters the Fat Lady while the poet enters a monastery and discovers the Buddha. Yet both arrive finally at the same destination. 'I wanted to be at my best, out of everyone's reach, in flight,' observes Joe (*LL*, p. 232).

Both Warren and Joe are romantic questers struck early in life by a similar vision of ideal femininity which becomes the driving force in their lives. But their errand is ultimately not a quest for the ideal woman but a 'lifelong search for the godhead' (*LL*, p. 291). Their search takes them finally to Loon Lake where their dedication is tested and corrupted. In one sense, they are like brothers, sons of the working class torn between their desire to justify their parents' lives and their own. Both Warren and Joe share the idea of killing Bennett but are deflected from their purpose and finally defeated. But in another sense, Warren is Joe's surrogate father who leaves the legacy of his writing – 'all that is left of me' – with the sentiment: 'You are what I would want my son to be' (*LL*, p. 205). Thus the ultimate conflict in the book is the struggle between two fathers, Penfield and Bennett, for possession of Joe's soul.

Richard King has suggested that *Loon Lake* is not simply a twentieth-century version of the quest for the ideal object: 'it is also a quest for legitimacy, for authorization of one's self as counting in the social order. Freud and Otto Rank gave us a name for the individual and cultural desire – the family romance. And what Doctorow has written is the American version of this collective family romance.'[38] But in the American version the pursuit of status and independence is transformed into the romance of the self-made man like *The Great Gatsby* and *Loon Lake*. Just as James Gatz renounces his working-class paternity when he changes his name to Jay

Gatsby, so Joseph Korzeniowski gives up his name to become the adopted son of F. W. Bennett.[39]

But there is this difference. Gatsby creates himself out of a corrupted Platonic ideal which is tenuously linked to an older and more innocent capacity for wonder. Intent on emphasizing the romantic aspect of his hero, Fitzgerald begins at the point where James Gatz has already become Jay Gatsby. On the other hand, Joe models himself on a debased cultural ideal which he both desires and resists. In his more sceptical portrait, Doctorow ends at the point where ordinary Joe from Paterson, New Jersey, has just become respectable Joseph Paterson Bennett, heir to Loon Lake. In its projection of the pursuit of the American dream, *Loon Lake* fills in the crucial years that *The Great Gatsby* all but leaves out.

Thus *Loon Lake* is the story of the self-made man who constructs himself from the outside in. Doctorow has said that Joe is 'someone who simply composes himself from the people in his experience' (*I*). His idea of style and self comes from the movies: Joe is an actor who becomes the role he plays. When talking for his life in the police station Joe discovers that the voice he improvises authenticates the identity he claims. His speech reveals him to be Bennett's son. He calls his performance 'a kind of industrial manufacture of my own' (*LL*, p. 263). So Joe assembles himself the way that Bennett's factory makes cars:

> And the more it went on, the more I believed it, taking this fact and that possibility and assembling them, then sending the results down the line a bit and adding another fact and dropping an idea on the whole thing and sending it on a bit for another operation, another bolt to the construction, my own factory of lies, driven by rage, Paterson Autobody doing its day's work. I was going to make it! (*LL*, pp. 263–4)

What he manufactures is a mechanical identity without a centre. In Doctorow's description, 'the image I use for Joe is emptiness' (*I*).

Joe's rise in the world is also his capitulation to the world. In the beginning, his quest for freedom leads him to scatter the money that he steals from the church and the carnival. His vitality resides in his resistance to the claims of authority and responsibility. Even after he arrives at Loon Lake, Joe struggles against its attractions, expressing his mocking contempt for the authority of wealth. But Joe's defiance is tinged with ambivalence. Even his outrageous gesture of signing the guest book – 'Joe. . . . Of Paterson. Splendid dogs. Swell company' (*LL*, p. 76) – is an ambiguous acknowledgement of the powerful attraction of wealth and status. Thus his convalescence at Loon Lake is partly a conversion. 'Something has leaked out through the stitches and some of the serious intention of the world has leaked in: like the sense of high stakes, the desolate chance of real destiny' (*LL*, p. 81).

What Joe discovers is the ubiquity of Bennett's empire which extends from Loon Lake all the way to Jacksontown. Capitalism is depicted, in Nicholas Shrimpton's phrase, as 'less the jungle than the web'.[40] Thus every act of rebellion on Joe's part is absorbed in a pattern of entanglement and acquiescence. His declaration to the police that he is Bennett's son is made to save his skin but it expresses the hidden truth. His final decision to return to Loon Lake may seem to him like an act of revenge but it is really a signal of surrender. George Stade has observed:

> In *Loon Lake*, Joe of Paterson (or Father–Son) triumphs over his adoptive father by becoming him, only worse. It is not a matter of co-option, as young men in Joe's position often complain, but of revenge through usurpation. In America, to generalize further, the sons win; they destroy the past only to preserve the worst of it in themselves, and thereby destroy the future. Such is Doctorow's variation on the conventional American success story.[41]

Though it may not be Doctorow's most formally perfect novel, *Loon Lake* is the most complex, ambitious and resonant of his works. Moreover, its assimilation of historical event and narrative innovation into a rich and original imaginative form suggests a growing mastery of the craft of fiction and, in particular, of the possibilities of the romance. But despite the novel's originality, it is still built out of elements found in his earlier fiction. As in *Ragtime* and *The Book of Daniel*, Doctorow creates twinned protagonists who function as *alter egos*. In all three novels one character resists his fate heroically and dies while the other survives but at great psychic cost. It is tempting to see in this pattern a schematic distribution of good and evil but Doctorow's artistry is more subtle than that. F. W. Bennett may resemble J. P. Morgan in his obsessions but he is capable of grief. Joe may, like Tateh, renounce his working-class heritage but both retain a consciousness of what has been lost. This is part of Penfield's legacy, as it was of Daniel's. Doctorow has called *Loon Lake* 'the most personally revealing' of his books and it is difficult to ignore the connection between the character who discovers his voice in order to construct his identity and the writer who must find a voice in order to compose his fiction. In writing *Drinks Before Dinner* and *Loon Lake*, Doctorow has both closed the circle of his earlier writing and opened a new phase of his career.

'LIVES OF THE POETS'

bless our poets who think they must make us suffer
  each other's feelings
in a world wide democracy of perception.

(American Anthem)

After the publication of *Loon Lake*, Doctorow once again turned away from the solitary pursuit of fiction to enter into collaborative ventures. First, he wrote the texts to J. C. Suarès's selection of photographs in *American Anthem*. This handsome coffee-table book provides a wry portrait of a divided society, in sharp contrast to the usual patriotic celebrations of Americana in such productions. Doctorow's responses to the dramatic photographs selected by Suarès are often sober and occasionally suggest the apocalyptic. For instance, in response to a picture of firemen in action, he writes: 'They move in their cumbersome uniforms with the gracelessness of a doomed species. The fires that are coming are too large for their simple trade. The fires that are coming are the complicated fires of abstractions and ideologies.' This dark tone was maintained in his second major project, a collaboration with the director Sidney Lumet on the film version of *The Book of Daniel* (see Appendix). Aside from this, Doctorow was also teaching creative writing, giving public readings and lending his support to various liberal political causes. All in all, a very public life for a writer who has always valued his privacy.

Soon he began to fashion a new fictional work which suggested a radical departure from his previous novels. After *Drinks Before Dinner* and *Loon Lake*, he was more confident in dealing with material that was both more personal and more contemporary. At the same time, he felt the need to explore further the possibilities of narrative form and language. But as the work progressed, it seemed to take one more unexpected turn. Alongside the novel, it turned out, he was creating something entirely new for him: a collection of short stories which were in some way intimately connected with each other and with the novel which he continued to write. This collection was published in 1984 under the title that he had originally considered for the novel, *Lives of the Poets*.

Once again, Doctorow took inspiration from his immediate environment. Just as *Ragtime* began with a description of his house in New Rochelle and *Loon Lake* was stimulated by a visit to the Adirondacks, where he had spent some childhood summers, so *Lives of the Poets* found its source in a new apartment in Greenwich Village which he took over as a part-time studio. Commuting between New Rochelle and New York and moving between the necessary isolation of the writer and the equally necessary sociability of the film collaborator and literary celebrity, Doctorow started to think about the situation of the writer oscillating between his public and private roles. Drawing on his own experience as well as the experiences of his contemporaries, Doctorow began to draw a portrait of his generation of artists in today's America. In its fragmented form, *Lives of the Poets* reflects the sense of division that Doctorow may have been feeling at the time.

Lives of the Poets is a slim volume consisting of six short stories and a novella. The stories are very different from one another in both form and language but they share certain recurrent images and ideas. Moreover, they gain a coherence and urgency from being written in a kind of continuous present. Yet the book lacks the obvious cohesion of the classic short-story cycles, possessing neither the geographical unity of Joyce's *Dubliners* or Sherwood Anderson's *Winesburg, Ohio*, nor the chronological development of Hemingway's *In Our Time*. Rather Doctorow creates an overall pattern of motifs which suggest synchronous relationships. He has likened his form to the phase music of composers like Steve Reich who replace the conventional linear progression or melody with a mosaic of themes. But in *Lives of the Poets* the pattern becomes meaningful when we encounter in the novella the voice of the author of the first six stories. Only when we have finished the book can we see all the connections. Then we are ready to read the stories again with a new understanding.

If this sounds overly calculated and abstract, the stories themselves have an intense narrative energy and an unsettling psychological reality that is haunting and disturbing. The stories vary in form from the conventional narrative of 'The Writer in the Family' to the experimental fragmentation of 'The Leather Man' which has no apparent plot at all. Several, like 'The Hunter' and 'The Foreign Legation', seem like psychological episodes more than ordinary stories. That is, much of *Lives of the Poets* is concerned with interior states of mind and with the nature of subjective reality. For instance, in 'Willi' an old man recalls an intense Oedipal experience from his childhood and questions the distinctions drawn between so-called subjective and objective reality:

> What an incredible achievement of fantasy is the scientific mind! We posit an empirical world, yet how can I be here at this desk in this room – and not be here? If memory is a matter of the stimulation of so many cells of the brain, the greater the stimulus – remorse, the recognition of fate – the more powerfully complete becomes the sensation of the memory until there is transfer, as in a time machine, and the memory is in the ontological sense another reality. (*LP*, p. 29)

This insistence on the power of imagination as an alternate but not subordinate reality may suggest the reflexive concerns of post-modern fictioneers like Robert Coover and John Barth, but Doctorow's interests lie elsewhere. Like other more conventional modernists – Saul Bellow and Philip Roth come to mind – Doctorow is concerned with the relationship between the inner reality that his characters shape and the outer reality which shapes them. In *Herzog*, Bellow portrayed the attempt of his protagonist to confront reality first with words and then by getting out of his mind. In *My Life as a Man*, Roth presented two stories written by his protagonist, Peter Tarnapol, and then produced the source of the stories in Tarnapol's autobiographical narrative. The form of *Lives of the Poets* owes something to both: like *Herzog*, it depicts the manifold cultural pressures that threaten to overwhelm the protagonist's mind; as in *My Life as a Man*, the stories are presented as the product of the authorial voice of the novella.

Moreover, like Bellow and Roth, Doctorow is concerned with the moral life of his characters. Haunted by the past and threatened by the present, they are transfixed between memory and reality. At the end of the novella, Doctorow quotes Rilke; interestingly enough, Roth uses the same lines at the conclusion of *The Breast*: '*Here there is no place that does not see you. You must change your life*' (*LP*, p. 131). But the call to self-transformation is not easily fulfilled. We cannot escape the accumulated weight of our own lives, the burden of our personal and collective history. Doctorow's conclusion brings little consolation: 'So my discovery at fifty is that this mortal rush to solitude is pandemic, that is the news I bring. It is not that everyone I know is fucked up, incomplete, unrealized. On the whole we are all quite game. It's life itself that seems to be wanting.' (*LP*, p. 85).

Tony Tanner has called the novels of Bellow and Roth 'fictionalized recall' to suggest the way these writers transform personal experience into fiction.[42] *Lives of the Poets* also builds on Doctorow's personal experience in a more direct way than his previous fiction. Like Doctorow himself, the protagonist of the title novella, Jonathan, is a Jewish writer who was raised in the Bronx, educated at Kenyon College and is the occupant of an apartment in Greenwich Village. But this does not mean that the book is autobiographical in the conventional sense. Though elements of the author's life appear in the novella, what is more important is that elements of his protagonist's life appear in the stories. Indeed, the pattern of the book depends upon our perception of the connections between the writer's life as expressed in the novella and *his* characters' lives as expressed in the stories. As Doctorow once observed, 'The novelist deals with his isolation by splitting himself in two, creator and documentarian, teller and listener, conspiring to pass on the collective wisdom in its own language, disguised in its own enlightened bias, that of the factual world' (*EC*, p. 21). Similarly, Jonathan projects parts of himself into his characters who share his own fears and desires. All writing is confessional and covert, real and imagined, the product of the writer's desire for isolation and of his need to communicate.

In the first story, 'The Writer in the Family', a young student, Jonathan, is called upon to convince his ageing grandmother that his recently deceased father is still alive by composing imaginary letters from him. Jonathan is chosen because he is the aspiring writer in the family. (The situation is partially autobiographical in that Jonathan's imaginative rendering in his letters of a West he has never seen recalls Doctorow's imaginative rendering of the West he had never seen in his first novel, *Welcome to Hard Times*.) But Jonathan's letters have a surprising effect on himself as well as others. To some family members, these fictions seem to make the dead man more real than when he was alive. To Jonathan, his constructions finally reveal something of his father's true nature which was hidden from him. The lies he creates disclose the truth about his own family situation.

'The Writer in the Family' is the longest, the most conventional and the most obviously 'autobiographical' of the stories. But it is also perhaps the most important because it contains the kernel of the most significant motifs running through the entire collection. Jonathan's discovery of the power of imagination is echoed in 'The Foreign Legation'. His description of family dynamics is elaborated in 'Willi'. His father's reputed failure and repressed desire for freedom resurface in 'The Leather Man'. Finally, the idea of historical continuity is identified with the recurring waves of immigration, from the Old World Jews at the turn of the century to the Third World refugees of the present time. The protagonist of 'The Foreign Legation' suffers 'a vision of the incessant migrations of mankind lapping the earth prehistorically, historically, and to the present moment' (*LP*, p. 61). These migrations symbolize the pattern of human metamorphosis and the rootlessness of modern life as well as the persistence of political upheavals: the burden of history.

The other five stories are all different in style, place and time but they share a similar concern for traumatic psychic experience. In 'The Water Works' the narrator witnesses the drowning of a child; in 'Willi' an old man recalls his betrayal of his parents. In 'The Hunter' a young teacher exploits her students' love as a shield against a threatening world; in 'The Foreign Legation' a detached young man has difficulty in separating his own aggressive urges from the reality of an explosive world. In 'The Leather Man' shadowy officials discuss how to cope with the reappearance of the alienated figure of the derelict. Unlike the hunted young woman and the estranged young man, the Leather Man can no longer hold the inner world of desire and the outer world of repression in neurotic balance. His cross is his vision. 'What is the essential act of the Leather Man?' asks the narrator. 'He makes the world foreign. He distances it. He is estranged. Our perceptions are sharpest when we're estranged. We can see the shape of things' (*LP*, pp. 71–2).

The Leather Man's sense of estrangement identifies him, of course, with the modern artist whose perceptions are also sharpest when he feels detached. But if the artist requires a sense of alienation for his work he also desires a feeling of harmony in his life. This is the dilemma that confronts Jonathan, the protagonist of the title novella and the putative author of the other stories. Jonathan seeks the 'dream life' in which mind and body harmonize in a union of self and ego. But this self-perfection ends in silence. He recognizes that his writing originates in dissatisfaction: his emotional frustrations, health anxieties and political fears generate his fiction. He recalls a poet friend who had systematically healed himself and then stopped writing. But instead of unifying himself, Jonathan projects his disparate parts into his stories, creating an artistic unity out of the fragments of personality.

Thus Jonathan confronts a paradox: the artist must isolate

himself to escape his isolation. (Doctorow once quoted John Berryman's definition of the writer as 'a person who sits alone in a room with the English language and tries to get his feelings right'.[43]) Seated in his room in Greenwich Village, Jonathan experiences a sense of isolation from his family and the outside world. This detachment, he insists, is necessary for his work. Yet his writing removes him from the claims of the world of which he feels a part; while he types out a paragraph he misses witnessing a man being arrested in the street beneath his window. No wonder he tells his wife that 'writing is like a sentence – it's a prison image' (*LP*, p. 92). And no wonder she tells him that he lives inside his neurosis. Thus Jonathan sympathizes with the alienation of the Leather Man and understands that 'between the artist and simple dereliction there is a very thin line' (*LP*, p. 96).

Lives of the Poets is concerned with this thin line between art and dereliction. In the most controversial parts of the book, Doctorow recounts the increasing dereliction of his generation of writers: the corruption of their work and the collapse of their private lives. As he once wryly noted, in America there are only two schools of literature – 'the school that vacations in eastern Long Island, and the school that summers in Martha's Vineyard'.[44] The tendency of writers to become part of the general culture of narcissism is a sign of their sense of failure or despair. 'Tell me,' demands a fellow writer of Jonathan at a cocktail party, 'is there a writer here who really believes in what he's doing? Does any of us have a true conviction for what he's writing? Do I? Do you?' (*LP*, p. 135).

Thus *Lives of the Poets* is both formal construction and jeremiad. In describing the isolation of the writer, Doctorow is echoing the artistic anxieties expressed by many of his contemporaries: that the subversive role of the writer has itself been subverted. Poets who once thought of themselves as the unacknowledged legislators of the world have been deprived of their ancient right to matter in a society whose tolerance masks indifference. 'Rather than making the culture we seem these days to be in it,' Doctorow has written. 'American culture suggests an infinitely expanding universe that generously accommodates, or imprisons, us all.'[45] Jonathan's apartment in Greenwich Village becomes a prison. In order to overcome his isolation he must accept the claims of the outside world and prepare to leave his room or share it. But the final image is of the writer writing, filling his daily quota, creating a legacy of words.

We can now see that all Doctorow's work has been concerned with the significance of the act of writing. All his protagonists have been poets, chroniclers and historians. Though not conventionally autobiographical, his characters have all been surrogates for the evolving artist: 'Emotionally, tonally, the topography of all these books is my own mental map of me.'[46] Jonathan may bear the nearest resemblance to his creator but he is closer still to his fictional predecessors. Like Daniel, he is filled with aggression and self-hate. Like Edgar, he is an inconsolable prophet. Like Penfield, he can see the comic absurdities of his own situation. Doctorow confesses to similar feelings of frustration:

> The condition of my working life as a novelist, as I experience it, is one of immense dissatisfaction with the form, with fiction itself, an impatience with what it has done, a terrible impatience with what I have done with it. The insufficiency of fiction and the need to reform it, I take as a metaphor for our need to transform our lives and remake ourselves.[47]

Lives of the Poets suggests a further development in Doctorow's writing both in its experimentation with form and in its exploration of personal experience. Doctorow has already called attention to the connection between the stories and his forthcoming novel; in fact, he has even suggested that the present volume may be read as a prologue to the work in progress. But whatever it will be like, we can be sure that the new novel will, like all his writing, keep faith with the hidden possibilities of American life and, like all significant art, offer us the thrill of new discovery and the shock of recognition.

APPENDIX: DOCTOROW ON FILM

The translation of a literary work into film is always problematical and so it has proved with Doctorow's novels. About the first, *Welcome to Hard Times*, there is not much to say. It was made into a film in 1967 (and released in England under the curious title, *Killer on a Horse*). Directed by Burt Kennedy and starring Henry Fonda as Blue, the movie simply failed to capture the quality of the novel: it was said to be one of the great disappointments of Fonda's career. Doctorow, who was not involved in the production, has called *Welcome to Hard Times* the second worst film ever made – after *Swamp Fire* with Johnny Weissmuller.

The story of the filming of *Ragtime* (1981) is a bit more complicated. The novel was optioned by the Italian producer, Dino De Laurentiis, who chose Robert Altman to direct it. The choice was an excellent one since Altman had demonstrated an affinity with Doctorow's vision in films like *McCabe and Mrs. Miller*. Doctorow was pleased because, in his opinion, Altman was a film-maker who thought like a novelist. He even spent some time with Altman during the filming of *Buffalo Bill and the Indians* and ended up making a brief appearance as one of President Cleveland's advisers.

Altman made elaborate plans for a 6-hour film and 10-hour television mini-series that would encompass all the strands of *Ragtime*. The concept was interesting – a kind of turn-of-the-century *Nashville* – if a bit extravagant. But Altman quarrelled with De Laurentiis about the editing of the film *Buffalo Bill* and the producer retaliated by firing him from the *Ragtime* project. Much to Doctorow's dismay, Milos Forman was hired to direct and Michael Weller was commissioned to write the screenplay.

Forman's ideas were more practical and less imaginative: he would try to keep the outlines of the book but concentrate on the story of Coalhouse Walker. This was all, it was felt, that could be treated in a film of standard length. Inevitably, this foreshortening involved major surgery. Most of the historical figures are deleted; only those involved in the Evelyn Nesbit scandal are elaborated. On the other hand, the role of a minor character, the New York Police Commissioner, is expanded to exploit the presence of veteran actor James Cagney. The result is a film that is far more conventional than the novel. Despite some good performances, atmospheric photography and an outstanding musical score, Forman's *Ragtime* is not a success.

The most obvious problem is that in focusing on the Coalhouse Walker story, Forman spoils the design of the novel. The interplay between fact and fiction is lost and, more surprisingly, Doctorow's vision of history, politics and culture is distorted. The most radical political change is in the character of Tateh. In the novel, he begins as a working-class radical whose health and family life have been ruined by poverty. His decision to discard the European dream of socialism for the American dream of success is treated by Doctorow as a complex act of betrayal and rejuvenation. In the film, he is a virile young man, devoid of political awareness, whose success as a pioneer movie director is not blemished by any ambivalence. By omitting any mention of Emma Goldman, the IWW, the Lawrence strike and socialism, Forman eliminates Doctorow's depiction of American radicalism, vulgarizes his portrayal of the working class and dilutes the political content of the novel.

Similarly, Forman's view of American culture is at odds with Doctorow's. In the novel, Doctorow uses ragtime and the movies as examples of how American culture evolved 'from the bottom up'. Thus when Coalhouse first comes to the house in

New Rochelle and is asked to perform, he plays Scott Joplin's 'Wall Street Rag'. In the identical scene in the film Coalhouse plays Chopin instead. It is as if Forman can only legitimize Coalhouse's art by having him prove that he can read 'high-brow' music as well. Forman's failure to make the connections between American society and popular culture which are so essential to the book suggests a paradox: if Doctorow consciously Americanized Kleist's novella then Forman deliberately Europeanized Doctorow's novel.

Doctorow was greatly disappointed with the adaptation of *Ragtime*. Thus when the time came to film *The Book of Daniel*, he chose to work closely with the director Sidney Lumet. *Daniel* (1983) seemed an unlikely subject for a Hollywood film but Lumet, with his New York Jewish background and his liberal political convictions, appeared a logical choice for director. From the beginning, the pair worked as a team, with Doctorow writing the screenplay, Lumet directing the actors, and both collaborating on the editing. Clearly, the film was not simply another commercial venture but a labour of love.

In many ways, the results are impressive. *Daniel* is certainly the most faithful rendering of a Doctorow novel on film. Doctorow's screenplay retains much of the language of the novel so that the aspirations and betrayals of the Old Left are depicted with a minimum of compromise. The scenes involving the Isaacsons in the 1940s and 1950s are often affecting, culminating in a grimly understated recreation of the execution. *Daniel* is a serious, almost solemn picture that makes few concessions to popular taste. Compared to *Reds* and *Ragtime*, its nearest competitors, it treats radical politics with care and complexity.

But there are problems. The film's stately pace lacks the energy of Daniel's narrative. The scenes in the past are often shot in a warm, golden hue that betrays a certain nostalgia. In comparison, the 1960s scenes, filmed in a cold, blue light, seem generalized and diffuse. The failure to portray the 'children' with the same care as the 'parents' unbalances the film and upsets the carefully constructed generational conflict which is at the heart of the novel. The most egregious error is the absence of Artie Sternlicht, the voluble spokesman for the New Left in the novel. (Apparently, a sequence involving Sternlicht was filmed but then rejected in the final version because of its poor quality.) Sternlicht's absence creates a hole at the centre of the picture which the viewer senses whether or not he has read the novel. Not simply the sense but the rhythm of the film is thrown off balance.

The absence of Sternlicht creates another problem. Without a counterweight, *Daniel* becomes a film about the parents: that is to say, a film about the Rosenbergs. Whereas the novel was concerned with 'the idea of the Rosenbergs' and did not have to face the question of guilt or innocence, the film, by concentrating on the past, emphasizes instead the trial and execution. Whereas the novel portrays the Isaacsons as victims of the Cold War, used cynically by both sides for propaganda purposes, the film seems to suggest that they were simply martyrs of Cold War hysteria. In the novel, a knowledgeable journalist tells Daniel, 'Between the FBI and the CP your folks never had a chance.' In the same scene in the film, this line is cut.

As it happened, *Daniel* appeared at the same time as Ronald Radosh and Joyce Milton's near definitive account, *The Rosenberg File*. This new book argued persuasively that Julius Rosenberg was involved in Soviet espionage but that there was insufficient evidence to convict his wife Ethel. In essence, the government framed Mrs Rosenberg as a way of getting her husband to talk. But the strategy backfired and two martyrs were created when the communists exploited the propaganda value of the trial after first abandoning its two victims. Since the film gave many people the impression of defending the Rosenbergs, it was attacked by critics as a distortion of the truth. Despite its very real virtues, *Daniel* was neither a critical nor a popular success.

In retrospect, it may be difficult for Doctorow to understand why he became involved in film projects in the first place. As a writer who delighted in the splendid isolation of his profession, Doctorow was unused to a medium which was characterized by collaboration, compromise and commercial considerations. No wonder that he once called film a 'regressive' medium. But as an artist fascinated by popular culture, he was not the first American writer to be attracted to the possibilities of expression in cinema. When asked why he continues to involve himself in a creative process that he finds frustrating, Doctorow simply shrugs his shoulders. But the fascination with film must surely run deep. Doctorow admits to having written screenplays of both *Ragtime* and, perhaps his most cinematic novel, *Loon Lake*. But, he says, almost with a sigh of relief, he doubts whether anyone could afford to turn *that* novel into a film.

NOTES

1 Nicholas Shrimpton, 'New Jersey Joe', *New Statesman*, 31 October 1980, p. 27.

2 Diane Johnson, 'Waiting for Righty', *New York Review of Books*, 6 November 1980, p. 18.

3 Victor S. Navasky, 'E. L. Doctorow: "I Saw a Sign"', *New York Times Book Review*, 28 September 1980, p. 44.

4 Richard Chase, *The American Novel and Its Tradition* (Baltimore, Md: Johns Hopkins University Press, 1980), p. 2.

5 Navasky, op. cit., p. 44.

6 Ronald Sukenick, 'The New Tradition in Fiction', in Raymond Federman (ed.), *Surfiction* (Chicago: Swallow Press, 1975), p. 36.

7 Doris Lessing, *The Golden Notebook* (New York: Ballantyne Books, 1973), p. 302.

8 Kurt Vonnegut, *Slaughterhouse-Five* (New York: Delacorte Press, 1969), p. 87.

9 Herbert G. Guttman, 'Whatever Happened to History?', *The Nation*, 21 November 1981, p. 554.

10 Martin Green, 'Nostalgia Politics', *American Scholar* (Winter 1975/76), pp. 841, 842.

11 Navasky, op. cit., p. 44.

12 Herbert Mitgang, 'Publishing: A Novel from E. L. Doctorow', *New York Times*, 5 September 1980, p. 20.

13 See John Clayton, 'Radical Jewish Humanism: The Vision of E. L. Doctorow', *EC*, pp. 109–19; and Sam Girgus, 'A True Radical History: E. L. Doctorow', in *The New Covenant: Jewish Writers and the American Idea* (Chapel Hill, NC: University of North Carolina Press, 1984), pp. 160–83.

14 Irving Howe, 'New Styles in "Leftism"', in *Steady Work* (New York: Harcourt, Brace & World, 1966), p. 47.

15   Nathaniel Hawthorne, *The Scarlet Letter* (New York: Norton, 1962), p. 31.
16   Philip French, *Westerns* (London: Secker & Warburg, 1973), p. 24.
17   Edwin Fussell, *Frontier: American Literature and the American West* (Princeton, NJ: Princeton University Press, 1965), p. 13.
18   Alan Trachtenberg, *The Incorporation of America* (New York: Hill & Wang, 1982), p. 17.
19   John G. Cawelti, *Adventure, Mystery, and Romance* (Chicago: University of Chicago Press, 1976), p. 193.
20   In an interview, Doctorow explained: 'With *Welcome to Hard Times*, it was just a sense of place which moved me tremendously. It was the landscape. I loved writing about it, imagining it. I had never been West. Halfway through the book, it occurred to me that maybe I ought to make sure it really was a possible terrain. I went to the library and read a geography book by Walter Prescott Webb – a marvelous book called *The Great Plains*. Webb said what I wanted to hear: no trees out there. Jesus, that was beautiful. I could spin the whole book out of one image. And I did' (*EC*, p. 39).
21   French, op. cit., p. 39.
22   Irving Howe, 'Radical Criticism and the American Intellectuals', in *Steady Work*, pp. 34–5.
23   Leslie Fiedler, 'The New Mutants', in *A Fiedler Reader* (New York: Stein & Day, 1977), p. 193.
24   Jerry Rubin, *Do It!* (New York: Simon & Schuster, 1970), pp. 90–1.
25   William O'Neill, *Coming Apart* (New York: Quadrangle Books, 1971), p. 279.
26   Ibid., p. 298.
27   Leslie Fiedler, 'Afterthoughts on the Rosenbergs,' in *A Fiedler Reader*, pp. 51–2.
28   Daniel clearly means the spheres of Magdeburg.
29   John Seelye, 'Doctorow's Dissertation', *New Republic*, 10 April 1976, p. 22.
30   See Barbara Foley, 'From *U.S.A.* to *Ragtime*: Notes on the Forms of Historical Consciousness in Modern Fiction', *EC*, pp. 158–78.
31   A photograph of a similar event was taken by Joseph Byron in 1900. Doctorow has altered the details of the occasion to suit his needs. See Martin W. Sandler, *This Was America* (Boston: Little, Brown, 1980), p. 131.
32   Heinrich von Kleist, 'Michael Kohlhaas', in *'The Marquise of O' and Other Stories*, trans. David Luke and Nigel Reeves (Harmondsworth: Penguin, 1978), p. 114.

33 Kathy Piehl, 'E. L. Doctorow and Random House: The Ragtime Rhythm of Cash', *Journal of Popular Culture* (Spring 1980), pp. 404–11.

34 Walter Clemons, 'Houdini, Meet Ferdinand', *Newsweek*, 14 July 1975, p. 73.

35 Johnson, op. cit., p. 19.

36 Richard King, 'Two Lights That Failed', *Virginia Quarterly Review* (Spring 1981), p. 344.

37 See David S. Gross, 'Tales of Obscene Power: Money and Culture, Modernism and History in the Fiction of E. L. Doctorow', *EC*, pp. 120–50.

38 King, op. cit., p. 343.

39 Several critics have noted that Doctorow has used Joseph Conrad's Polish name for his hero. But the significance of this naming remains unclear. Perhaps Doctorow merely wished to pay tribute to a writer whose works have acted as an influence but whose politics differed significantly from his own.

40 Shrimpton, op. cit., p. 27.

41 George Stade, 'Types Defamiliarized', *The Nation*, 27 September 1980, p. 286.

42 Tony Tanner, *City of Words* (London: Jonathan Cape, 1976), p. 295.

43 Leonard Russ, 'After "Ragtime", A New Rhythm', *New York Times Book Review*, 3 April 1977, p. 3.

44 E. L. Doctorow, 'Living in the House of Fiction', *The Nation*, 22 April 1978, p. 460.

45 Ibid., p. 459.

46 Hilary Mills, 'Creators on Creating: E. L. Doctorow', *Saturday Review* (October 1980), p. 46.

47 Doctorow, 'Living in the House of Fiction', p. 461.

BIBLIOGRAPHY

WORKS BY E. L. DOCTOROW

Novels

Welcome to Hard Times. New York: Simon & Schuster, 1960.
Published in England as *The Bad Man from Bodie*. London: André
Deutsch, 1961.
Big as Life. New York: Simon & Schuster, 1964.
The Book of Daniel. New York: Random House, 1971. London:
Macmillan, 1972.
Ragtime. New York: Random House, 1975. London: Macmillan,
1975.
Loon Lake. New York: Random House, 1980. London: Macmillan,
1980.

Short fiction

Lives of the Poets. New York: Random House, 1984. London:
Michael Joseph, 1985.

Play

Drinks Before Dinner. New York: Random House, 1979.

Non-fiction

'Writers and Politicians', *New York Times*, 11 April 1976, section 4,
p. 17.
'The New Poetry'. *Harper's Magazine* (May 1977), pp. 92–5.
'False Documents'. *American Review*, 26 (November 1977), pp.
215–32. Reprinted in shortened form in Richard Trenner (ed.),

E. L. Doctorow: Essays and Conversations, pp. 16–30. Princeton, NJ: Ontario Review Press, 1983.

'Living in the House of Fiction'. *The Nation*, 22 April 1978, pp. 459–61.

'The Language of Theater'. *The Nation*, 2 June 1979, pp. 637–8. Reprinted in revised form as the Introduction to *Drinks Before Dinner*.

'Words into Rhinestones'. *New York Times*, 19 March 1980, p. 27.

'The Rise of Ronald Reagan'. *The Nation*, 19–26 July 1980, pp. 1, 82–4.

'Art Funding for the Artist's Sake'. *The Nation*, 4 July 1981, pp. 12–13. Reprinted as 'For the Artist's Sake', in Richard Trenner (ed.), *E. L. Doctorow: Essays and Conversations*, pp. 13–15. Princeton, NJ: Ontario Review Press, 1983.

American Anthem, with photographs selected by J. C. Saurès and text by E. L. Doctorow. New York: Stewart, Tabori & Chang, 1982.

Introduction to *Sister Carrie* by Theodore Dreiser. New York: Bantam Classics, 1982.

'On the Brink of 1984'. *Playboy Magazine*, 30 (February 1983), pp. 79–80, 156–62.

'It's a Cold War World Out There, Class of '83'. *The Nation*, 2 July 1983, pp. 6–7.

SELECTED CRITICISM OF E. L. DOCTOROW

Books

Trenner, Richard (ed.). *E. L. Doctorow: Essays and Conversations*. Princeton, NJ: Ontario Review Press, 1983. A collection of essays by, interviews with and critical articles on E. L. Doctorow.

Interviews

Levine, Paul. 'The Writer as Independent Witness'. In *E. L. Doctorow: Essays and Conversations*, pp. 57–72.

McCaffery, Larry. 'A Spirit of Transgression'. In Tom Le Clair and Larry McCaffery (eds), *Anything Can Happen: Interviews with Contemporary American Novelists*. Urbana, Ill.: University of Illinois Press, 1983. Reprinted in *E. L. Doctorow: Essays and Conversations*, pp. 31–47.

Mills, Hilary. 'Creators on Creating: E. L. Doctorow'. *Saturday Review* (October 1980), pp. 44–8.

Mitgang, Herbert. 'Publishing: A Novel from E. L. Doctorow'. *New York Times*, 5 September 1980, p. 20.

Navasky, Victor S. 'E. L. Doctorow: "I Saw a Sign"'. *New York Times Book Review*, 28 September 1980, pp. 44–5.

Russ, Leonard. 'After "Ragtime", A New Rhythm'. *New York Times Book Review*, 3 April 1977, p. 3.

Trenner, Richard. 'Politics and the Mode of Fiction'. *Ontario Review*, 16 (Spring/Summer 1982), pp. 5–16. Reprinted in *E. L. Doctorow: Essays and Conversations*, pp. 48–56.

Articles

Arnold, Marilyn. 'History as Fate in E. L. Doctorow's Tale of a Western Town'. *South Dakota Review*, 18 (Spring 1980), pp. 53–63. Reprinted in *E. L. Doctorow: Essays and Conversations*, pp. 207–16.

Brienza, Susan. 'Doctorow's *Ragtime*: Narrative as Silhouettes and Syncopation'. *Dutch Quarterly Review of Anglo-American Letters*, 11 (1981–2), pp. 97–103.

Chances, Ellen. 'The Reds and *Ragtime*: The Soviet Reception of E. L. Doctorow'. In *E. L. Doctorow: Essays and Conversations*, pp. 151–7.

Clayton, John. 'Radical Jewish Humanism: The Vision of E. L. Doctorow'. In *E. L. Doctorow: Essays and Conversations*, pp. 109–19.

Cooper, Barbara. 'The Artist as Historian in the Novels of E. L. Doctorow'. *Emporia State Research Studies*, 29, pp. 5–44.

Ditsky, John. 'The German Source of *Ragtime*: A Note'. *Ontario Review*, 4 (Spring/Summer 1976), pp. 84–6. Reprinted in *E. L. Doctorow: Essays and Conversations*, pp. 179–81.

Emblidge, David. 'Marching Backward into the Future'. *Southwest Review*, 62 (Autumn 1977), pp. 397–408.

Estrin, Barbara. 'Surviving McCarthyism: E. L. Doctorow's *The Book of Daniel*'. *Massachusetts Review*, 16 (Summer 1975), pp. 577–87. Reprinted in *E. L. Doctorow: Essays and Conversations*, pp. 196–206.

Foley, Barbara. 'From *U.S.A.* to *Ragtime*: Notes on the Forms of Historical Consciousness in Modern Fiction'. *American Literature*, 50 (March 1978), pp. 85–105. Reprinted in *E. L. Doctorow: Essays and Conversations*, pp. 158–78.

Girgus, Sam. 'A True Radical History: E. L. Doctorow'. In *The New Covenant: Jewish Writers and the American Idea*. Chapel Hill, NC: University of North Carolina Press, 1984, pp. 160–83.

Gross, David S. 'Tales of Obscene Power: Money and Culture, Modernism and History in the Fiction of E. L. Doctorow'.

E. L.

Marx)'.
Massachusetts Review, 21 (Fall 1980), pp. 487–501.

Levine, Paul. 'The Conspiracy of History: E. L. Doctorow's *The Book of Daniel*'. *Dutch Quarterly Review of Anglo-American Letters*, 11 (1981–2), pp. 82–96. Reprinted in *E. L. Doctorow: Essays and Conversations*, pp. 182–95.

Saltzman, Arthur. 'The Stylistic Energy of E. L. D   ow'. In *E. L. Doctorow: Essays and Conversations*, pp. 73–1(

Seelye, John. 'Doctorow's Dissertation'. *New Republic*, 10 April 1976, pp. 21–3.

Stark, John. 'Alienation and Analysis in Doctorow's *The Book of Daniel*'. *Massachusetts Review*, 16 (Summer 1975), pp. 101–10.

Strout, Cushing, 'Historizing Fiction and Fictionalizing History: The Case of E. L. Doctorow'. *Prospects* (1980), pp. 423–37.

Book reviews

Clemons, Walter. 'Houdini, Meet Ferdinand'. *Newsweek*, 14 July 1975, pp. 73–4.

Green, Martin. 'Nostalgia Politics'. *American Scholar* (Winter 1975/76), pp. 841–5.

Johnson, Diane. 'Waiting for Righty'. *New York Review of Books*, 6 November 1980, pp. 18–20.

King, Richard. 'Two Lights That Failed'. *Virginia Quarterly Review*, 57 (Spring 1981), pp. 341–50.

Kauffmann, Stanley. 'A Central Vision'. *Saturday Review*, 26 July 1975, pp. 20–2.

—— 'Wrestling Society for a Soul'. *New Republic*, 5 June 1971, pp. 25–7.

Shrimpton, Nicholas. 'New Jersey Joe'. *New Statesman*, 31 October 1980, p. 27.

Stade, George. Review of *Ragtime*. *New York Times Book Review*, 6 July 1975, pp. 1–2.

—— 'Types Defamiliarized'. *The Nation*, 27 September 1980, pp. 285–6.

Starr, Kevin. Review of *Welcome to Hard Times*. *Saturday Review*, 6 September 1975, pp. 25–7.